The High-Performance Entrepreneur

The High-Performance Entrepreneur

12 Essential Strategies to Supercharge Your Startup Business

The Convenient Coach Series, Volume I

David P. Hale, PhD

Contributing Authors:

Barbara Lyngarkos, MBA
Timothy P. Maxwell II
Michael B. Meek, MSM
Robert T. Uda, MBA

iUniverse, Inc.
New York   Bloomington   Shanghai

The High-Performance Entrepreneur
12 Essential Strategies to Supercharge Your Startup Business

Copyright © 2008 by David P. Hale

iUniverse books may be ordered through booksellers or by contacting:

iUniverse
1663 Liberty Drive
Bloomington, IN 47403
www.iuniverse.com
1-800-Authors (1-800-288-4677)

Because of the dynamic nature of the Internet, any Web addresses or links contained in this book may have changed since publication and may no longer be valid.

The information, ideas, and suggestions in this book are not intended to render professional advice. Before following any suggestions contained in this book, you should consult your personal accountant or other financial advisor. Neither the author nor the publisher shall be liable or responsible for any loss or damage allegedly arising as a consequence of your use or application of any information or suggestions in this book.

ISBN: 978-0-595-49647-1 (pbk)
ISBN: 978-0-595-50095-6 (cloth)
ISBN: 978-0-595-61192-8 (ebk)

Printed in the United States of America

This book is dedicated to The Highest Power, God, who blessed me with the strength to survive the toughest journey of my life, stage-four throat cancer. It is through the energy, strength, focus, and passion He infuses me with that I am able to live in the High Performance (HiPer) Zone.

To my wife, Dawn, who through her love and understanding of whom I am and what I wish to achieve, empowers me to greatness. It was through her constant support that this book was able to evolve.

To my biggest cheerleaders, my parents, Richard and Ethel Hale, who taught me that I could achieve anything despite facing the toughest odds.

To my contributing authors go my unending thanks for staying on track, meeting deadlines, and making this project a reality. You are truly living in the HiPer Zone!

Lastly, to my high school guidance counselor who motivated me to become who I am today by telling me I would be lucky to obtain a job pumping gas. Luckily, he was *wrong*!

Contents

Preface

After having had many conversations with friends, clients, and my university students concerning the trials and tribulations of starting and running their entrepreneurial ventures, it was suggested to me to put my experience and advice to paper.

The main issue that seems to plague the success rate of many entrepreneurs today is that their business success, or lack thereof, is directly correlated to their level of preparation (Passion + Preparation = High Performance). Often, entrepreneurs allow the excitement of starting a new venture to take center stage. Unfortunately, this enthusiasm can obscure the need to plan appropriately, which includes writing a business and marketing plan, developing a Web presence, obtaining the proper licenses or zoning authorizations, and acquiring the required knowledge of how to hire, manage, and train employees.

I have started several entrepreneurial ventures, starting at the age of ten with a lawn care business. In the early 1970s, I was making $250 per week mowing lawns, raking leaves, and shoveling plenty of snow in the winter. Today, I run a global business-consulting firm, *HiPer Solutions*, specializing in business development and human resource strategic coaching and training.

In between projects, I teach business development and organizational psychology courses for Webster University, Columbia, SC, and Northcentral University in Prescott Valley, AZ. The passion for learning I witness in my students is what I also see in entrepreneurs who have planned every business development move. These High-Performance Entrepreneurs have also told me they, in turn, lose their passion and zeal when working on a project they have not planned.

With so many entrepreneurial dreams being shattered everyday, it is my hope that the performance strategies outlined in this book will become the catalyst in assisting the entrepreneurial nation to supercharge their business startups. I am sure that by putting these strategies into action, you will not only begin to develop the passion and zeal others feel, but you will also be well on your way to developing yourself into a *High-Performance Entrepreneur*!

Introduction

This book is about living your dreams and seeing your hard work pay off. It is about a particular dream, The American Dream of Entrepreneurial Financial Freedom. It is also a book about knowing that you can get there from here—that is, knowing how to properly plan your entrepreneurial dream in order to develop a sustainable venture. It is about discovering who you are, what you believe you are capable of building, and whom those key strategic people around you are who can help you get there.

Every year, thousands of people start businesses. But how many of those business ventures will remain operational in a year? Three years? Five years? Those who are unable to handle the stresses of entrepreneurship will fall by the wayside, never to fulfill their dreams. If we looked closer, we would more than likely find that what most business failures have in common is poor planning. Poor planning can include inadequate idea formation, insufficient market planning, lack of financial resources, or a lack of knowledge about how to obtain the greatest exposure in the market.

Many times, those who were unable to get going just ran out of steam. They did not possess the required sustainability, energy, passion, or—as I have coined it—the "HiPer" (High-Performance) attitude. Through my own business experience and in coaching entrepreneurs around the world, I have found that many people do not have the faintest idea of what they are doing, what they got themselves into, or how they are going to reach their dream.

This book is about you, the entrepreneur who knows what he wants. Someone who knows he possesses the burning desire to live his dreams. This book is not about going it alone or attempting to build a sustainable business without proper planning. If you are a person who believes you can build a sustainable business all by yourself, then this book is not for you. This book is for the winners who *know* they have the burning desire, energy, and ability to properly plan for the long haul. If this sounds like you, then you embody the spirit of The High Performance Entrepreneur.

When entrepreneurs want to develop their dreams, it is important to develop structures and procedures to support the process of creating something new. Think of yourself as a house builder. In order to build a house that will stand properly, you must first level the ground and build a strong foundation. Without a proper foundation or strong beams, the house will fall. Your business is no different. You must hone your ideas, know that you have adequate finances, properly write a business and marketing plan, know where you are going to operate from, and find your strategic partners or network that will help you along the way.

While reading the pages you are holding, you will find a bank of resources and learn what is needed to reach your goals, develop a sustainable business, and achieve your ultimate dream.

In the first strategy, you will hone your business ideas and determine what finances you have and will need. Honing your ideas includes developing your entrepreneurial goal into one that excites you and provides its own sustainable source of motivation. You will learn how to align your entrepreneurial ideas with your personal values in order to make your business goals part of who you are. This first strategy will assist you in developing the strong foundation the High-Performance Entrepreneur needs to develop sustainability.

In the remaining strategies, you will learn how to develop the daily routines needed to maintain your path. You will create action plans to use as visual displays to keep you on track. Through self-assessments, you will orient yourself around daily, weekly, and annual reporting schedules so you will know how close you are to your goals.

Lastly, you will learn strategies to locate those key strategic people, through networking, who will assist you in locating clients, help keep you on track, and provide you with the momentum you need to develop into The High Performance Entrepreneur.

This book is a compilation of entrepreneurial strategies developed by several thought leaders. The team I have brought together is made up of people who live The High Performance Entrepreneurial life. They are people who have not only developed several multi-million dollar entrepreneurial businesses, but also coach forward by assisting others throughout the world in doing the same.

Think of this book as your personal business coach who will provide you with the tools needed to create your venture. Keep this book near to you, in order to deliver the hip-pocket training you will need throughout the day.

This book is the beginning of a bigger dream of mine, to bring high-performance coaching to many areas within the business world. *The High-Performance Entrepreneur: 12 Essential Strategies to Supercharge Your Startup Business* is the first volume in the *Convenient Coach Series*. Future volumes will focus on management, training, corporate coaching, Internet marketing, and many other business topics.

[Strategy 1]

The High-Performance Entrepreneur Plans and Forecasts

David P. Hale, PhD

The beginning is the most important part ...
Plato

In business, there are no guarantees. There is simply no way to eliminate all the risks associated with starting a small business—but you can improve your chances of success with good planning, preparation, and insight. Start by evaluating your strengths and weaknesses as a potential owner and manager of a small business. Carefully consider each of the following questions:

Are you a self-starter? It will be entirely up to you to develop projects, organize your time, and follow through on details.

How well do you get along with different personalities? Business owners need to develop working relationships with a variety of people including customers, vendors, staff, bankers, and professionals such as lawyers, accountants, or consultants. Can you deal with a demanding client, an unreliable vendor, or a cranky receptionist if your business interests demand it?

How good are you at making decisions? Small business owners are required to make decisions constantly—often quickly, independently, and under pressure.

Do you have the physical and emotional stamina to run a business? Business ownership can be exciting, but it is also a lot of work. Can you face six or seven twelve-hour workdays every week?

How well do you plan and organize? Research indicates that poor planning is responsible for most business failures. Good organization of financials, inventory, schedules, and production can help you avoid many pitfalls.

Is your drive strong enough? Running a business can wear you down emotionally. Some business owners burn out quickly from having to carry all the responsibility for the success of their business on their own shoulders. Strong motivation will help you survive slowdowns and periods of burnout.

How will the business affect your family? The first few years of business startup can be hard on family life. It is important for family members to know what to expect and for you to be able to trust that they will support you during this time. There also may be financial difficulties until the business becomes profitable, which could take months or years. You may have to adjust to a lower standard of living or put family assets at risk in the short-term.

What follows in this chapter is a compilation of several topics you will revisit in later chapters. In this first chapter, you will get your bearings and ideas straight, and you will compile some critical numbers you will need later on. For now, let's dig in!

Getting Started Checklist

Before starting out, list your reasons for wanting to go into business. Ask yourself these questions and check off each one *Yes* or *No* when answered:

	Yes	No
You want to be your own boss.	____	____
You want financial independence.	____	____
You want creative freedom.	____	____
You want to fully use your skills and knowledge.	____	____

Next, you need to determine what business is "right for you." Ask yourself these questions and check off each one *Yes* or *No* when answered:

	Yes	No
What do I like to do with my time?	____	____
What technical skills have I learned or developed?	____	____
What do others say I am good at?	____	____
How much time do I have to run a successful business?	____	____
Do I have any hobbies or interests that are marketable?	____	____

Then you should identify the niche your business will fill. Conduct the necessary research to answer these questions and check off each one *Yes* or *No* when answered:

	Yes	No
Is my idea practical and will it fill a need?	____	____
Who is my competition?	____	____
What is my business advantage over existing firms?	____	____
Can I deliver a better quality service?	____	____
Can I create a demand for my business?	____	____

The final step before developing your plan is the pre-business checklist. You should ensure that you have answered these questions. Mark them off as you answer them:

What business am I interested in starting?	_____
What services or products will I sell?	_____
Where will I be located?	_____
What skills and experience do I bring to the business?	_____
What will be my legal structure? (see overview below)	_____
What will I name my business?	_____
What equipment or supplies will I need?	_____
What insurance coverage will be needed?	_____
What financing will I need?	_____
How will I compensate myself?	_____

Your answers will help you create a focused, well-researched business plan that should serve as a blueprint. It should detail how the business will be operated, managed, and capitalized.

Why Small Businesses Fail

Success in business is never automatic. It isn't strictly based on luck—although a little never hurts. It depends primarily on the owner's foresight and organization. Even then, of course, there are no guarantees. Starting a small business is always risky, and the chance of success is slim. According to the U.S. Small Business Administration (SBA), roughly 50 percent of small businesses fail within the first years.

In his book *Small Business Management*, Michael Ames gives the following reasons for small business failure:

- Lack of experience
- Poor planning
- Insufficient capital (money)
- Poor location
- Poor inventory management
- Over-investment in fixed assets
- Poor credit arrangements
- Personal use of business funds
- Unexpected growth

On the Upside

It is true that there are many reasons not to start your own business. However, for the right person, the advantages of business ownership far outweigh the risks.

- You will be your own boss.
- Hard work and long hours directly benefit you, rather than increasing profits for someone else.
- Earning and growth potential are far greater.
- A new venture is as exciting as it is risky.
- Running a business provides endless challenge and opportunities for learning.

Do You Have What It Takes?

Learn the characteristics and habits of creative, successful entrepreneurs. Many highly successful entrepreneurs have similar traits and characteristics. Learn what these are and what you can do to improve on your own.

What Do Successful Entrepreneurs Have in Common?

- Persistence
- Desire for immediate feedback
- Inquisitiveness
- Strong drive to achieve
- High energy level
- Goal-oriented behavior
- Independent
- Demanding
- Self-confident
- Calculated risk taker
- Creative
- Innovative
- Vision

- Commitment
- Problem-solving skills
- Tolerance for ambiguity
- Strong integrity
- Highly reliable
- Personal initiative
- Ability to consolidate resources
- Strong management
- Organizational skills
- Competitive
- Change agent
- Tolerance for failure
- Desire to work hard

Many entrepreneurs also had a role model to influence them early on and parents who were entrepreneurs. Two traits necessary for successful entrepreneurs are creativity and innovation.

What Is Creativity?

Creativity is the ability to come up with new ideas and different ways to solve problems that provide opportunities.

Characteristics of Creative People

- Bright
- Adaptable
- High self-esteem
- Challenge oriented
- Idea oriented
- Inquisitive
- Curious

Can you improve your creativity? Yes! How?

Gather as much information as you can (read, talk with experts, etc.) and brainstorm. Just think about the problem or issue until an idea comes to you. Is the solution reasonable? If so, try it. If not, keep thinking. If you tried out an idea, did it work? If so, great! If not, begin the process over again. Do not put barriers on your mind. Put these steps to use.

What Is an Innovation?

An innovation is something that is invented, like the CD, or something that is created from an existing idea or product (e.g., Super Wal-Mart).

Where do innovative ideas come from?

- Unsatisfied customers
- Demographic changes in society
- Luck
- Imagination
- Vision
- Problem solving

Remember:

- Look for new ideas.
- Keep it simple.
- Start small.
- Try, try, try again.

Checklist for Starting a High-Performance Business

Owning a business is the dream of many Americans … starting that business converts your dreams into reality. However, there is a gap between dreams and reality. Your dreams can only be achieved with careful planning. As an entrepreneur, you will need a plan to avoid pitfalls, to achieve your goals, and to build a profitable business.

This checklist is designed to help you prepare a comprehensive business plan and determine if your idea is feasible, to identify questions and problems you will face in converting your idea into reality, and to prepare for starting a business. It has seven key components:

- Identify Your Reasons
- Self-Analysis
- Personal Skills and Experience
- Finding a Niche
- Market Analysis
- Planning Your Startup
- Finances

Each component is comprehensive and is designed to prepare you for self-employment. In addition, each component includes a self-analysis of your responses as well as a menu of supporting resources.

Identify Your Reasons

As a first and often overlooked step, ask yourself why you want to own your own business. Check the reasons that apply to you.

	Yes	No
Freedom from the nine-to-five daily work routine	——	——
Being your own boss	——	——
Doing what you want when you want to do it	——	——
Improving your standard of living	——	——
Boredom with your present job	——	——
Having a product or service for which you feel there is a demand	——	——

Some reasons are better than others are, but none are wrong; however, be aware that there are trade-offs. For example, you can escape the 9 AM–5 PM daily grind, but you may be replacing it with a 6 AM–10 PM routine.

A Self-Analysis

Personal Characteristics

Going into business requires certain personal characteristics. This portion of the checklist deals with you—the individual. These questions require serious thought. Try to be objective. Remember, it is your future at stake!

	Yes	No
Are you a leader?	___	___
Do you like to make your own decisions?	___	___
Do others turn to you for help in making decisions?	___	___
Do you enjoy competition?	___	___
Do you have willpower and self-discipline?	___	___
Do you plan ahead?	___	___
Do you like people?	___	___
Do you get along well with others?	___	___

Personal Conditions

This next group of questions, though brief, is vitally important to the success of your plan. It covers the physical, emotional, and financial strains you will encounter in starting a new business.

	Yes	No
Are you aware that running your own business may require working twelve-sixteen hours a day, six days a week and maybe even Sundays and holidays?	_____	_____
Do you have the physical stamina to handle the workload and schedule?	_____	_____
Do you have the emotional strength to withstand the strain?	_____	_____
Are you prepared, if needed, to temporarily lower your standard of living until your business is firmly established?	_____	_____
Is your family prepared to go along with the strains they too must bear?	_____	_____
Are you prepared to lose your savings?	_____	_____

Finding a Niche

Small businesses range in size from a manufacturer with many employees and millions of dollars in equipment to the lone window washer with a bucket and a sponge. Obviously, the knowledge and skills required for these two extremes are far apart, but they have one thing in common—each has found a business niche and is filling it.

The most crucial problem you will face in your early planning will be to find your niche and determine the feasibility of your idea. "Get into the right business at the right time" is very good advice, but following that advice may be difficult. Many entrepreneurs plunge into a business venture so blinded by the dream that they fail to thoroughly evaluate its potential.

Before you invest time, effort, and money, the following exercise will help you separate sound ideas from those bearing a high potential for failure.

Identify and briefly describe the business you plan to start.

_____

_____

_____

_____

Identify the product or service you plan to sell.

_____

_____

_____

_____

	Yes	No
Does your product or service satisfy an unfilled need?	____	____
Will your product or service serve an existing market in which demand exceeds supply?	____	____
Will your product or service be competitive based on quality, selection, price, or location?	____	____

Answering yes to any of these questions means you are on the right track; a negative answer means the road ahead could be rough.

Market Analysis

For a small business to be successful, the owner must know the market. To learn the market, you must analyze it, a process that takes time and effort. You do not have to be a trained statistician to analyze the marketplace, nor does the analysis have to be costly.

Analyzing the market is a way to gather facts about potential customers and to determine the demand for your product or service. The more information you gather, the greater your chances of capturing a segment of the market. Know the market before investing your time and money in any business venture.

These questions will help you collect the information necessary to analyze your market and determine if your product or service will sell.

	Yes	No
Do you know who your customers will be?	____	____
Do you understand their needs and desires?	____	____
Do you know where they live?	____	____
Will you be offering the kind of products or services that they will buy?	____	____
Will your prices be competitive in quality and value?	____	____
Will your promotional program be effective?	____	____
Do you understand how your business compares with your competitors?	____	____
Will your business be conveniently located for the people you plan to serve?	____	____
Will there be adequate parking facilities for the people you plan to serve?	____	____

Planning Your HiPer Startup

So far, this checklist has helped you identify questions and problems you will face converting your idea into reality and determining if your idea is feasible. Through self-analysis, you have learned of your personal qualifications and deficiencies, and through market analysis, you have learned if there is a demand for your product or service.

The following questions are grouped according to function. They are designed to help you plan your business startup.

Name and Legal Structure

	Yes	No
Have you chosen a name for your business?	___	___
Have you chosen to operate as sole proprietorship, partnership, or corporation?	___	___

Your Business and The Law

A person in business is not expected to be a lawyer, but each business owner should have a basic knowledge of laws affecting the business. Following are some of the legal matters you should be acquainted with.

Protecting Your Business

	Yes	No
Do you know which licenses and permits you may need to operate your business?	___	___
Do you know the business laws you will have to obey?	___	___
Do you have a lawyer who can advise you and help you with legal papers?	___	___
Are you aware of:		
• Occupational Safety and Health Administration requirements?	___	___
• Regulations covering hazardous material?	___	___
• Local ordinances covering signs, snow removal, etc.?	___	___
• Federal Tax Code provisions pertaining to small business?	___	___
• Federal regulations on withholding taxes and social security?	___	___

It is becoming increasingly important that attention be given to security and insurance protection for your business. There are several areas that should be covered. Have you examined the following categories of risk protection?

	Yes	No
Fire	⎯⎯	⎯⎯
Theft	⎯⎯	⎯⎯
Robbery	⎯⎯	⎯⎯
Vandalism	⎯⎯	⎯⎯
Accident Liability	⎯⎯	⎯⎯

Business Premises and Location

	Yes	No
1. Have you found a suitable building in a location convenient for your customers?	⎯⎯	⎯⎯
2. Can the building be modified for your needs at a reasonable cost?	⎯⎯	⎯⎯
3. Have you considered renting or leasing with an option to buy?	⎯⎯	⎯⎯
4. Will you have a lawyer check the zoning regulations and lease?	⎯⎯	⎯⎯

Merchandise

	Yes	No
Have you decided what items you will sell or produce or what service(s) you will provide?	⎯⎯	⎯⎯
Have you made a merchandise plan based upon estimated sales to determine the amount of inventory you will need to control purchases?	⎯⎯	⎯⎯
Have you found reliable suppliers who will assist you in the startup?	⎯⎯	⎯⎯
Have you compared the prices, quality, and credit terms of suppliers?	⎯⎯	⎯⎯

Business Records

	Yes	No
Are you prepared to maintain complete records of sales income and expenses, accounts payable and receivables?	____	____
Have you determined how to handle payroll records, tax reports, and payments?	____	____
Do you know what financial reports should be prepared and how to prepare them?	____	____

Finances

A large number of small businesses fail each year. There are a number of reasons for these failures, but one of the main reasons is insufficient funds. Too many entrepreneurs try to start and operate a business without sufficient capital (money). To avoid this pitfall, first review your situation by analyzing these three questions:

1. How much money do you have?   _____
2. How much money will you need to start your business?   _____
3. How much money will you need to stay in business?   _____

Use the following table (personal financial statement) to answer the first question:

Table 1 — Personal Financial Statement

Personal Financial Statement
_____, 20 ____

ASSETS

Cash on hand	$_____
Savings account	$_____
Stocks, bonds, securities	$_____
Accounts/notes receivable	$_____
Real estate	$_____
Life insurance (cash value)	$_____
Automobile/other vehicles	$_____
Other liquid assets	$_____
TOTAL ASSETS	$_____

LIABILITIES

Accounts payable	$_____
Notes payable	$_____
Contracts payable	$_____
Taxes	$_____
Real estate loans	$_____
Other liabilities	$_____
TOTAL LIABILITIES	$_____

Table 2 (startup cost estimate) will help you answer the second question: how much money will you need to start your business? The chart is for a retail business. Items will vary for service, construction, and manufacturing businesses. The answer to the third question (How much money will you need to stay in business?) must be divided into two parts: immediate costs and future costs.

Table 2—Startup Cost Estimate

Decorating, remodeling	$_____
Fixtures, equipment	$_____
Installing fixtures, equipment	$_____
Services, supplies	$_____
Beginning inventory cost	$_____
Legal, professional fees	$_____
Telephone utility deposits	$_____
Insurance	$_____
Signs	$_____
Advertising for opening	$_____
Unanticipated expenses	$_____
TOTAL STARTUP COSTS	$_____

From the moment the door to your new business opens, a certain amount of income will undoubtedly come in. However, this income should not be projected in your operating expenses. You will need enough money available to cover costs for at least the first three months of operation. Table 3 (estimate for one month) will help you project your operating expenses on a monthly basis.

Table 3—Estimate for One Month

Your living costs	$_____
Employee wages	$_____
Rent	$_____
Advertising	$_____
Supplies	$_____
Utilities	$_____
Insurance	$_____
Taxes	$_____
Maintenance	$_____
Delivery/transportation	$_____
Miscellaneous	$_____
TOTAL EXPENSES FOR ONE MONTH	$_____

Now multiply the total of table 3 by three. This is the amount of cash you will need to cover operating expenses for three months. Deposit this amount in a savings account before opening the doors to your business. Use it for only those purposes listed in the above table because this money will ensure that you will be able to continue in business during the crucial early stages.

Table 4—Total for Three Months

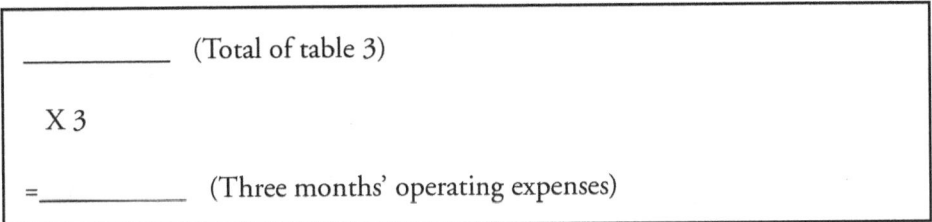

_____ (Total of table 3)

X 3

=_____ (Three months' operating expenses)

By adding the total startup costs (table 2) to the total expenses for three months (table 4), you can learn what the estimated costs will be to start up and operate your business for three months. By now subtracting the cash available (table 1), you can determine the amount of additional financing you may need, if any.

Table 5—Additional Financing Needed

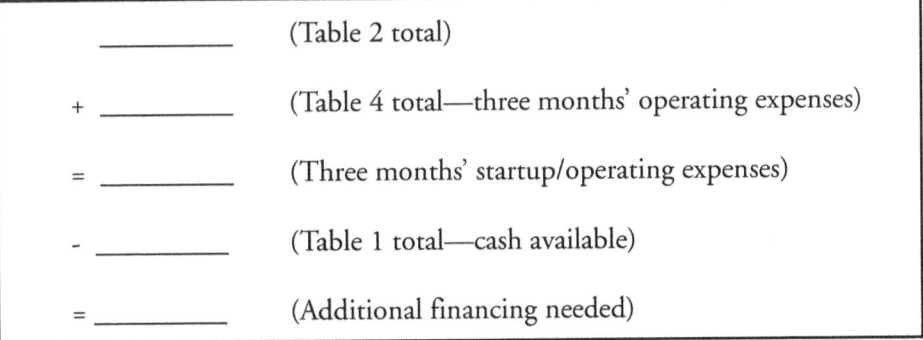

_____ (Table 2 total)

+ _____ (Table 4 total—three months' operating expenses)

= _____ (Three months' startup/operating expenses)

- _____ (Table 1 total—cash available)

= _____ (Additional financing needed)

After Startup

The primary source of revenue for your business will be from sales or services performed, but your sales will vary from month to month because of seasonal patterns and other factors. Therefore, it is important to determine if your monthly sales will produce enough income to pay each month's bills.

Conclusion

Without a doubt, preparing an adequate plan is the most important step in starting a new business. A comprehensive plan will be your guide to managing a successful business and *is paramount to your business success*. Your plan must contain all the pertinent information about your business; it must be well written, factual, and organized in a logical sequence. Moreover, it should not contain any statement that cannot be supported. We will cover this further in strategy 10.

If you have carefully answered all the questions on the checklists and completed all the worksheets, you have seriously thought about your goal. Nevertheless, there may be some things you feel you need to know more about.

Owning and running a business is a continuous learning process. Research your idea and do as much as you can yourself, but do not hesitate to seek help from people who can tell you what you need to know. Consider hiring a business coach (www.hipercoaching.com) or obtain assistance from your local SBA office, Small Business Development Center (SBDC), or the Service Corps of Retired Executives (SCORE).

[Strategy 2]

The High-Performance Entrepreneur Gets Organized

David P. Hale, PhD

The creation of a thousand forests is in one acorn.
Ralph Waldo Emerson

Naming Your Business

There is more to naming your business than just coming up with something that sounds good and you happen to like. Thought must be given to state and local requirements and making sure you do not infringe upon the rights of someone else's business name.

Legal Requirements and Implications

Picking a name for your business requires much more than just creativity and a working knowledge of your target market. First, you will need to decide which business structure you will use, since each structure has its own peculiarities. For example, many states require a sole proprietor to use his own name for the business name unless he formally files another name as a trade name or fictitious name. Alternatively, some states will file your sole proprietorship under your own name, but allow for the use of another business name.

Similarly, you will need to determine whether your trade name will be the same as the full legal name of your business. Usually, this depends on what organization structure you choose. Of equal importance is finding out whether your name or a very similar name is being used by another business, and if so, what rights they may or may not have to use the name in the area where you do business. Keep in mind that some businesses only file trademarks within their locality, so it is possible that the same name can be used elsewhere.

Search and Registration

Trade names can be registered through your state's Secretary of State office (www.statelocalgov.net/50states-secretary-state.cfm), and for wider marketplace protection, through the U.S. Patent and Trademark Office (USPTO) (www.uspto.gov/main trademarks.htm). You should first use the USPTO's online system to search all state and federal trademark registers to see if your proposed name is being used.

Domain Names

For many businesses that operate on the Web, trade names are synonymous with domain names, such as Amazon.com and Monster.com. Domain names are not registered through state or local government; rather, they can be obtained through numerous online businesses, most of which will allow you to conduct a name search prior to purchase to make sure your chosen name is not taken. Conduct a search at www.HiPerWebSolutions.com. Often, people register domain names as an investment. They do not intend to operate a business by the name, but are waiting for someone like you to come along and buy it from them for more than they paid. This domain name owner's identification and contact information is available when you conduct the search at www.HiPerWebSolutions.com.

Choosing Your Form of Ownership

Many factors must be considered when choosing the best form of business ownership or structure. The choice you make can have an impact on multiple aspects of your business, including taxes, liability, ownership succession, and others.

One of the first decisions that you will have to make as a business owner is how the company should be structured. This decision will have long-term implications, so consult with an accountant and attorney to help you select the form of ownership that is right for you. In making a choice, you will want to take into account the following:

- Your vision regarding the size and nature of your business
- The level of control you wish to have
- The level of structure you are willing to deal with
- The business' vulnerability to lawsuits
- Tax implications of the different ownership structures
- Expected profit (or loss) of the business

- Whether or not you need to reinvest earnings into the business
- Your need for access to cash out of the business for yourself

Sole Proprietorships

The vast majority of small businesses start out as sole proprietorships. These businesses are owned by one person, usually the individual who has day-to-day responsibilities for running the operation. Sole proprietors own all the assets of the business and the profits generated by it. They also assume complete responsibility for any of its liabilities or debts. In the eyes of the law and the public, you are one in the same with the business.

Advantages of a Sole Proprietorship

- Easiest and least expensive form of ownership to organize.
- Sole proprietors are in complete control, and within the parameters of the law, may make decisions as they see fit.
- Sole proprietors receive all income generated by the business to keep or reinvest.
- Profits from the business flow directly to the owner's personal tax return.
- The business is easy to dissolve, if desired.

Disadvantages of a Sole Proprietorship

- Sole proprietors have unlimited liability and are legally responsible for all debts against the business. Their business and personal assets are at risk.
- Sole proprietors may be at a disadvantage in raising funds and are often limited to using funds from personal savings or consumer loans.
- Sole proprietors may have a hard time attracting high-caliber employees or those that are motivated by the opportunity to own a part of the business.
- Some employee benefits such as owner's medical insurance premiums are not directly deductible from business income (only partially deductible as an adjustment to income).

Federal Tax Forms for Sole Proprietorship (www.irs.gov)

(This reflects only a partial list and some may not apply.)

- Form 1040: Individual Income Tax Return
- Schedule C: Profit or Loss from Business (or Schedule C-EZ)

- Schedule SE: Self-Employment Tax
- Form 1040-ES: Estimated Tax for Individuals
- Form 4562: Depreciation and Amortization
- Form 8829: Expenses for Business Use of your Home
- Employment Tax Forms

Partnerships

In a partnership, two or more people share ownership of a single business. Like sole proprietorships, the law does not distinguish between the business and its owners. The partners should have a legal agreement that sets forth how decisions will be made, how profits will be shared, how disputes will be resolved, how future partners will be admitted to the partnership, how partners can be bought out, and what steps will be taken to dissolve the partnership when needed. Yes, it is hard to think about a breakup when the business is just getting started, but many partnerships split up at crisis times, and unless there is a defined process, there will be even greater problems. They also must decide upfront how much time and capital each will contribute.

Advantages of a Partnership

- Partnerships are relatively easy to establish; however, time should be invested in developing the partnership agreement.
- With more than one owner, the ability to raise funds may be increased.
- The profits from the business flow directly through to the partners' personal tax returns.
- Prospective employees may be attracted to the business if given the incentive to become a partner.
- The business usually will benefit from partners who have complementary skills.

Disadvantages of a Partnership

- Partners are jointly and individually liable for the actions of the other partners.
- Profits must be shared with others.
- Since decisions are shared, disagreements can occur.

- Some employee benefits are not deductible from business income on tax returns.
- The partnership may have a limited life; it may end upon the withdrawal or death of a partner.

Types of Partnerships That Should Be Considered

1. **General Partnership:** Partners divide responsibility for management and liability as well as the shares of profit or loss according to their internal agreement. Equal shares are assumed unless there is a written agreement that states differently.

2. **Limited Partnership and Partnership with Limited Liability:** Limited means that most of the partners have limited liability (to the extent of their investment) as well as limited input regarding management decisions, which generally encourages investors for short-term projects or for investing in capital assets. This form of ownership is not often used for operating retail or service businesses. Forming a limited partnership is more complex and formal than that of a general partnership.

3. **Joint Venture:** Acts like a general partnership, but is clearly for a limited period of time or a single project. If the partners in a joint venture repeat the activity, they will be recognized as an ongoing partnership and will have to file as such, as well as distribute accumulated partnership assets upon dissolution of the entity.

Federal Tax Forms for Partnerships (www.irs.gov)

(This reflects only a partial list and some may not apply.)

- Form 1065: Partnership Return of Income
- Form 1065 K-1: Partner's Share of Income, Credit, Deductions
- Form 4562: Depreciation
- Form 1040: Individual Income Tax Return
- Schedule E: Supplemental Income and Loss
- Schedule SE: Self-Employment Tax
- Form 1040-ES: Estimated Tax for Individuals
- Employment Tax Forms

Corporations

A corporation chartered by the state in which it is located is considered by law to be a unique entity, separate and apart from those who own it. A corporation can be taxed, it can be sued, and it can enter into contractual agreements. The owners of a corporation are its shareholders. The shareholders elect a board of directors to oversee the major policies and decisions. The corporation has a life of its own and does not dissolve when ownership changes.

Advantages of a Corporation

- Shareholders have limited liability for the corporation's debts or judgments against the corporation.
- Generally, shareholders can only be held accountable for their investment in stock of the company. (Note: officers can be held personally liable for their actions, such as the failure to withhold and pay employment taxes.)
- Corporations can raise additional funds through the sale of stock.
- A corporation may deduct the cost of benefits it provides to officers and employees.
- A corporation can elect S corporation status if certain requirements are met. This election enables the company to be taxed similar to a partnership.

Disadvantages of a Corporation

- The process of incorporation requires more time and money than other forms of organization.
- Corporations are monitored by federal, state, and some local agencies, and as a result may have more paperwork to comply with regulations.
- Incorporating may result in higher overall taxes. Dividends paid to shareholders are not deductible from business income; thus, it can be taxed twice.

Federal Tax Forms for Regular Corporations (www.irs.gov)

(This reflects only a partial list and some may not apply.)

- Form 1120 or 1120-A: Corporation Income Tax Return
- Form 1120-W: Estimated Tax for Corporation
- Form 8109-B: Deposit Coupon

- Form 4625: Depreciation
- Employment Tax Forms
- Other forms as needed for capital gains, sale of assets, alternative minimum tax, etc.

Subchapter S Corporations

This election enables the shareholder to treat the earnings and profits as distributions and have them pass through directly to their personal tax return. The catch here is that the shareholder, if working for the company, and if there is a profit, must pay him/herself wages and must meet standards of "reasonable compensation." This can vary by geographical region as well as occupation, but the basic rule is to pay yourself what you would have to pay someone to do your job, as long as there is enough profit. If you do not do this, the IRS can reclassify all of the earnings and profit as wages, and you will be liable for all of the payroll taxes on the total amount.

Federal Tax Forms for Subchapter S Corporations (www.irs.gov)
(This reflects only a partial list and some may not apply.)

- Form 1120S: Income Tax Return for S Corporation
- 1120S K-1: Shareholder's Share of Income, Credit, Deductions
- Form 4625: Depreciation
- Employment Tax Forms
- Form 1040: Individual Income Tax Return
- Schedule E: Supplemental Income and Loss
- Schedule SE: Self-Employment Tax
- Form 1040-ES: Estimated Tax for Individuals
- Other forms as needed for capital gains, sale of assets, alternative minimum tax, etc.

Comparison of Legal Entities

	Sole Proprietorship	Partnership	Corp.	Subchapter S. Corp.
Difficulty and cost to form	Low	Low to Moderate	High	High
Difficulty and cost to maintain	Low	Low	High	High
Risk of owner liability	High	High	Low	Low
Difficulty of tax preparation	Low	Moderate	High	High
Flexibility of ownership; bringing in new owners	Low	Moderate	High	Low
Cost of terminating business	Low	High	High	High

Limited Liability Company (LLC)

The LLC is a relatively new type of hybrid business structure that is now permissible in most states. It is designed to provide the limited liability features of a corporation and the tax efficiencies and operational flexibility of a partnership. Formation is more complex and formal than that of a general partnership.

The owners are members, and the duration of the LLC is usually determined when the organization papers are filed. The time limit can be continued, if desired, by a vote of the members at the time of expiration. LLCs must not have more than two of the four characteristics that define corporations: limited liability to the extent of assets, continuity of life, centralization of management, and free transferability of ownership interests.

Federal Tax Forms for LLC

An LLC is taxed as a partnership in most cases; corporation forms must be used if there are more than two of the four corporate characteristics, as described above.

In summary, deciding the form of ownership that best suits your business venture should be given careful consideration. Use your key advisers to assist you in the process.

Special Structures

The following business structures are available in some states, but not all.

Limited Liability Partnership (LLP)

LLPs are organized to protect individual partners from personal liability for the negligent acts of other partners or employees not under their direct control. LLPs are not recognized by every state, and those that do sometimes limit LLPs to organizations that provide a professional service, such as medicine or law, for which each partner is licensed. Partners report their share of profits and losses on their personal tax returns. Check with your Secretary of State's office to see if your state recognizes LLPs, and if so, which occupations qualify.

Professional Service Corporation (PS)

A PS must be organized for the sole purpose of providing a professional service for which each shareholder is licensed. The advantage here is limited personal liability for shareholders. This option is available to certain professionals, such as doctors, lawyers, and accountants. Check with your Secretary of State's office to find out which occupations qualify.

Limited Partnership (LP)

LPs have complex formation requirements and require at least one general partner who is fully responsible for partnership obligations and normal business operations. The LP also requires at least one limited partner, often an investor, who is not involved in everyday operations and is shielded from liability for partnership obligations beyond the amount of their investment. LPs do not pay tax, but must file a return for informational purposes; partners report their share of profits and losses on their personal returns.

Non-Profit Corporations

These are formed for civic, educational, charitable, and religious purposes and enjoy tax-exempt status and limited personal liability. Non-profit corporations are managed by a board of directors or trustees. Assets must be transferred to another non-profit group if the corporation is dissolved.

Obtaining a D&B D-U-N-S Number

It is also important to update your company information in various data sources. Perhaps the most important of these is Dun & Bradstreet. A D&B D-U-N-S Number is a unique nine-digit sequence recognized as the universal standard for identifying and keeping track of over seventy million businesses worldwide. If you have not done so, you should register for your D-U-N-S Number, and if you are registered, update your information. Other data sources include federal, state, and local Web resource sites where your business may monitor contracting opportunities, vendor Web sites, and other e-commerce-related sites. It is important to change authorized users on these accounts, as well as all signature authorities, both with e-commerce and traditional brick-and-mortar businesses and entities, such as your bank.

Registration in the Central Contractor Registration system, or CCR, is equally as important as registering for a D-U-N-S Number. For any small business owner interested in doing business with the federal government, you must be registered in the CCR. The CCR is the primary database of the Department of Defense (DoD), NASA, Department of Transportation (DoT), and Department of Treasury. Both current and potential government vendors are required to register in CCR to be awarded contracts with DoD, NASA, DoT, and Department of Treasury. Vendors are required to complete a one-time registration to provide basic information relevant to procurement and financial transactions. Vendors must update or renew their registrations annually to maintain an active status.

CCR validates the vendor's information and electronically shares the secure and encrypted data with the federal agencies' finance offices to facilitate paperless payments through electronic funds transfer. Additionally, CCR shares the data with several government offices. Registration does not guarantee business with the government.

The PRO-Net database maintained by the SBA has been integrated into the CCR, so small business owners interested in becoming part of PRO-Net must now register in CCR. Like the CCR, PRO-Net becomes the tool that federal agencies and prime contractors use to identify small businesses to engage as subcontractors, in addition to being a tool for marketing your small concern. To register, go to www.ccr.gov and follow the prompts. You will need a D-U-N-S Number before you can register in CCR.

Conclusion

No other step is more important than starting your entrepreneurial venture with a legal name. This goes for both the physical name of your business and any domain names you may use. Checking with both your Secretary of State's office and the USPTO (www.uspto.gov/main trademarks.htm) will start you on the right path. Ensuring that you obtain the proper business license from your city, county, or town hall is additionally an important step.

Choosing the proper business structure will provide you with the proper operational guidelines and allow you the appropriate tax advantages. Fully understanding all of the risks, advantages, disadvantages, and liabilities for your chosen business structure will allow your business to stand on the proper legal footing.

[Strategy 3]

The High-Performance Entrepreneur Decides to Buy, Start, or Franchise

David P. Hale, PhD

My own business always bores me to death; I prefer other people's.

Oscar Wilde

Starting a business requires you to complete a number of steps and make some key decisions. As part of your overall plan, you will need to select a location, decide on a business structure, and obtain the necessary licenses and permits. In addition, determining whether to purchase an existing business or a franchise may be another option for you to consider.

Never think you can do it all alone! One of the best ways to insulate you against business failure is to find and work with a business coach or mentor, someone with business experience who can guide and assist you. One resource is www. hipercoaching.com.

Buying a Business

Once you decide to start a business, often the next decision is whether to buy an existing business or start a new venture from scratch. No matter which you decide, there are advantages and disadvantages to both.

Many entrepreneurs find the idea of running a small business appealing, but lose their motivation after dealing with business plans, investors, and legal issues associated with new startups. For those disheartened by such risky undertakings, buying an existing business is often a simpler and safer alternative.

Advantages

One of the main reasons for buying an existing business is the drastic reduction in startup costs, time, money, and energy. Additionally, cash flow may start immediately, thanks to existing inventory and accounts receivable. Other benefits include existing customer goodwill and easier financing opportunities, if the business has a positive record of accomplishment.

Disadvantages

The biggest block to buying a small business is the initial purchasing cost. As the business concept, customer base, brands, and other fundamental work have already been done, the financial cost of acquiring an existing business is usually greater than starting from scratch. Other possible disadvantages include hidden problems associated with the business and receivables that are valued at the time of purchase, but later turn out to be non-collectable. Prior research will pay dividends and help you avoid these problems.

Purchase Research

When you have found a business that you would like to buy, it is important to conduct a hard, objective investigation. Look into every aspect of the business, verifying whether the owner's stated reasons for selling are legitimate; double-check every detail for accuracy.

Professional Help

A qualified attorney should be consulted to help review the legal and organizational documents of the business you are planning to purchase. An accountant can help complete a proper evaluation of the financial condition of the business. To find an attorney in your area, use the American Bar Association's legal directory at www.abanet.org.

Letter of Intent

A letter of intent usually creates a non-binding offer to purchase the business and is usually needed in order for the seller to provide sensitive information about the business. It should spell out the proposed price, terms, and conditions for the sale of the business. The letter should also state that either side may revise or quit for any reason.

Confidentiality Agreement

Often required by the seller, a confidentiality agreement indicates that you will not use the information about the seller's business for any purpose other than deciding whether or not to buy.

Contracts and Leases

It is important to discover all the obligations that the business is responsible for. Also, be aware that you may have to work with the current property owner to assume any existing lease on the business premises or negotiate a new lease. If you acquire an existing lease from another lessee, you may have to pay the previous lessee for the privilege. The cost of acquiring your lease may be amortized over the remaining term of the lease.

Financial Statements and Tax Returns

Examine the financial statements from the business for at least the past three to five years. Also make sure that the statements are accompanied by an audit letter from a reputable CPA firm. Do not accept a simple financial review by the business itself. Review the tax returns from the past three to five years. This will assist in determining the profitability of the business as well as whether any tax liability is remaining.

Important Documents

You should review the following existing business documents when deciding whether or not to purchase a business:

- Real and personal property documents
- Bank accounts
- Customer lists
- Sales records
- Supplier/purchaser list
- Contracts
- Advertisement materials
- Inventory receipts/lists
- Organization charts
- Payroll, benefits, and employee pension/profit-sharing info

- List of employees
- Certifications by federal, state, or local
- List of owners

Determining Value

A realistic business valuation requires more than merely looking at last year's financial statement; it requires a thorough analysis of several years of the business operation and an opinion about the industry outlook, the economy, and how the company will compete.

Most people believe that a business should be sold for *Fair Market Value*. The term *Fair Market Value* is defined by the IRS as:

> *"The price at which the property would change hands between a willing buyer and willing seller when the former is not under any compulsion to buy and the latter is not under any compulsion to sell, both parties having reasonable knowledge of relevant facts"* (Revenue Ruling 59–60).

There are several different methods to determine a fair and equitable price for an existing business. The following lists a few methods used to determine the price:

- *Capitalized Earning Approach*—This method refers to the return on the investment that is expected by an investor.
- *Excess Earning Method*—This method is similar to the capitalized earning method, except that it splits off return on assets from other earnings.
- *Cash Flow Method*—This method is usually used when attempting to determine how much of a loan the cash flow of the business will support. The adjusted cash flow is used as a benchmark to measure the firm's ability to service debt.
- *Tangible Assets (Balance Sheet) Method*—This method values the business by the tangible assets.
- *Value of Specific Intangible Assets Method*—This method is based upon the buyer's buying a wanted intangible asset versus creating it. This method also takes into consideration valuing the goodwill of the business.

Sales Agreement

The sales agreement is the key document when buying the business assets or stock of a corporation. It is important to make sure the agreement is accurate and contains all the terms of the purchase. It would be a good idea to have an attorney review this document. It is in this agreement that you should define everything that you intend to purchase of the business, assets, customer lists, intellectual property, and goodwill.

The following is a checklist of items that should be addressed in the agreement:

- Names of seller, buyer, and business
- Background information
- Assets being sold
- Purchase price and allocation of assets
- Covenant not to compete
- Any adjustments to be made
- The terms of the agreement and payment terms
- List of inventory included in the sale
- Compliance with the bulk sales laws of the state
- Any representation and warranties of the seller
- Any representation and warranties of the buyer
- Determination as to the access to any business information
- Determination as to the running of the business prior to closing
- Contingencies
- Possibilities of having the seller continue as a consultant
- Fees, including brokers fees
- Date of closing

Licenses and Permits

Most businesses need licenses and permits to operate. The type of license or permit you need depends on your industry and the state in which you are located. License and permit requirements also affect where you locate your business, how much you will have to spend for remodeling, and whether or not you will have to provide off-street parking.

Zoning Requirements

It is important to check the zoning requirements for the area where you are acquiring your business. The zoning requirements may affect the type of business that you are intending to operate in a particular area.

Environmental Concerns

If you are acquiring real property along with the acquisition of the business, it is important to check the environmental regulations in the area.

Closing Checklist

It is important during the closing to make sure that you have legal counsel available to review all documentation necessary for the transfer of the business.

The following items should be addressed in a closing:

- *Adjust Purchase Price*—This would take care of prorated items such as rent, utilities, and inventory up to the time of closing.

- *Review Documents Required to be Provided by the Seller*—These would be a corporate resolution approving the sale, evidence that a corporation is in good standing, or any tax releases that may have been promised by the seller. Check with your local Department of Corporations or Secretary of State.

- *Signing Promissory Note*—In some cases, the seller will carry back financing. So, have an attorney review any note documentation.

- *Security Agreements*—These may be necessary if you are going to finance your purchase. A Security Agreement lists the assets that will be used for security as a promise for payment of the loan.

- *UCC Financing Statements*—These documents are recorded with the Secretary of State in the state you have purchased your business. Again, these documents are necessary if you are going to finance your business.

- *Lease*—If you have agreed to assume an existing lease, you will be required to execute the assumption. Make sure that you have the property owner's concurrence to assumption of the lease. You may have negotiated a new lease with the property owner instead of assuming the existing lease.

- *Vehicles*—If the purchase includes vehicles, you may have to execute the transfer documents for the vehicles. You can check with your local Department of Motor Vehicles to determine the correct procedure and necessary forms.

- *Bill of Sale*—The bill of sale will be proof of the sale of the business and will transfer the ownership of the other tangible business assets not specifically transferred on their own.

- *Patents, Trademarks, and Copyrights*—You may need to execute the necessary forms if part of the transaction.

- *Franchise*—You may have to execute franchise documents if the purchase of the business was a franchise.

- *Closing or Settlement Sheet*—The closing or settlement sheet will list all financial aspects of the transaction. Everything listed on the settlement should have been negotiated prior to the closing, so there should be no surprises.

- *Covenant Not to Compete*—It is a good idea to have the seller execute this agreement. This will help add to the success of your operation of the business without any interference from the previous owner.

- *Consultation/Employment Agreement*—If the seller has agreed to remain on for an amount of time, this documentation would be necessary.

- *IRS Form 8594, Asset Acquisition Statement*—This document will indicate how the purchase was allocated among the various assets. It is important for your tax return.

- *Bulk Sale Laws*—Make sure that all bulk sale laws have been complied with in the transfer of the business assets.

Franchising

An important step in the small business startup process is deciding whether or not to go into business at all. Each year, thousands of potential entrepreneurs are faced with this difficult decision. Due to the risk and work involved in starting a new business, many new entrepreneurs choose franchising as an alternative to starting a new, independent venture from scratch.

One of the biggest mistakes you can make is to hurry into business; it is important to understand your reasons for going into business and determine if owning a business is right for you. This was discussed in strategy 1.

If you are concerned about the risk involved in a new independent business venture, then franchising may be the best business option for you. However, remember that hard work, dedication, and sacrifice are essential to the success of any business venture, including franchising.

What Is Franchising?

A franchise is a legal and commercial relationship between the owner of a trademark, service mark, trade name, or advertising symbol and an individual or group wishing to use that identification in a business. The franchise governs the method of conducting business between the two parties. Generally, a franchisee sells goods or services supplied by the franchiser or that meet the franchiser's quality standards.

Franchising is based on mutual trust between the franchiser and franchisee. The franchiser provides the business expertise (marketing plans, management guidance, financing assistance, site location, training, etc.) that otherwise would not be available to the franchisee. The franchisee brings the entrepreneurial spirit and drive necessary to make the franchise a success.

There are primarily two forms of franchising:

- Product and trade name franchising
- Business format franchising

In the simplest form, a franchiser owns the right to the name or trademark and sells that right to a franchisee. This is known as product and trade name franchising. The more complex form, business format franchising, involves a broader ongoing relationship between the two parties. Business format franchises often provide a full range of services, including site selection, training, product supply, marketing plans, and even assistance in obtaining financing.

Shopping at a Franchise Exposition

Attending a franchise exposition allows you to view and compare a variety of franchise possibilities. Keep in mind that exhibitors at the exposition primarily want to sell their franchise systems. Be cautious of salespersons who are interested in selling a franchise that you are not interested in.

Before you attend, research what type of franchise best suits your investment limitations, experience, and goals. When you attend, comparison shop for the opportunity that best suits your needs and ask questions.

Know How Much You Can Invest

An exhibitor may tell you how much you can afford to invest or that you cannot afford to pass up this opportunity. Before beginning to explore investment options, consider the amount you feel comfortable investing and the maximum amount you can afford.

Know What Type of Business Is Right for You

An exhibitor may attempt to convince you that an opportunity is perfect for you. Only you can make that determination. Consider the industry that interests you before selecting a specific franchise system. You should answer the following questions before proceeding:

- Have I considered working in that industry before?
- Can I see myself engaged in that line of work for the next twenty years?

Do You Have the Necessary Background or Skills?

If the industry does not appeal to you or you are not suited to work in that industry, do not allow an exhibitor to convince you otherwise. Spend your time focusing on those industries that offer a more realistic opportunity.

Comparison Shop

Visit several franchise exhibitors engaged in the type of industry that appeals to you. Listen to the exhibitors' presentations and discussions with other interested consumers. Get answers to the following questions:

- How long has the franchiser been in business?
- How many franchised outlets currently exist?
- Where are they located?
- How much is the initial franchise fee and any additional startup costs? Are there any continuing royalty payments? How much?
- What management, technical, and ongoing assistance does the franchiser offer?
- What controls does the franchiser impose?

Exhibitors may offer you incentives, prizes, free samples, or free dinners if you attend a promotional meeting later that day or over the next week to discuss the franchise in detail. Do not feel compelled to attend; rather, consider these meetings as one way to acquire more information and ask additional questions. Be prepared to walk away from any promotion if the franchise does not suit your needs.

Get Substantiation for any Earnings Representations

Some franchisers may tell you how much you can earn if you invest in their franchise system or how current franchisees in their system are performing. Be careful. The FTC requires that franchisers who make such claims provide you with written substantiation. Make sure you ask for and obtain written substantiation for any income projections or income and profit claims. If the franchiser does not have the required substantiation or refuses to provide it to you, consider its claims to be suspect.

Take Notes

It may be difficult to remember each franchise exhibit. Bring a pad and pen to take notes. Get promotional literature that you can review. Take the exhibitors' business cards so you can contact them later with any additional questions.

Avoid High-Pressure Sales Tactics

You may be told that the franchiser's offering is limited, that there is only one territory left, or that this is a one-time reduced franchise sales price. Do not feel pressured to make any commitment. Legitimate franchisers expect you to comparison shop and investigate their offering. A good deal today should be available tomorrow.

Study the Franchiser's Offering

Do not sign any contract or make any payment until you have the opportunity to investigate the franchiser's offering thoroughly. The *Federal Trade Commission's (FTC) Franchise Rule* requires the franchiser to provide you with a disclosure document containing important information about the franchise system. Study the disclosure document. Take time to speak with current and former franchisees about their experiences. As investing in a franchise can entail a significant commitment, you should have an attorney review the disclosure document and franchise contract along with having an accountant review the company's financial disclosures.

Before Selecting a Franchise System

Before investing in a particular franchise system, carefully consider how much money you have to invest, your abilities, and your goals. The following checklist may help you make your decision.

My Investment

- How much money can I invest?
- How much money can I afford to lose?
- Will I purchase the franchise by myself or with partners?
- Will I need financing and, if so, where can I obtain it?
- Do I have a favorable credit rating?
- Do I have savings or additional income to live on while starting a franchise?

My Abilities

- Does the franchise require technical experience or relevant education, such as auto repair, home and office decorating, or tax preparation?
- What skills do I have? Do I have computer, bookkeeping, or other technical skills?
- What specialized knowledge or talents can I bring to a business?
- Have I ever owned or managed a business?

My Goals

- What are my goals?
- Do I require a specific level of annual income?
- Am I interested in pursuing a particular field?
- Am I interested in retail sales or performing a service?
- How many hours am I willing to work?
- Do I want to operate the business by myself or hire a manager?
- Will franchise ownership be my primary source of income or will it supplement my current income?
- Would I be happy operating the business for the next twenty years?
- Would I like to own several outlets or only one?

Investigating Franchise Offerings

Before investing in any franchise system, be sure to get a copy of the franchiser's disclosure document. Sometimes this document is called a *Franchise Offering Circular*. Under the FTC's Franchise Rule, you must receive the document at least ten business days before you are asked to sign any contract or pay any money to the franchiser. You should read the entire disclosure document; make sure you understand all of the provisions. The following outline will help you to understand key provisions of typical disclosure documents as well as ask questions about the disclosures. Get clarification or an answer to your concerns before you invest.

Business Background

The disclosure document identifies the executives of the franchise system and describes their prior experience. Consider not only their general business background, but their experience in managing a franchise system. Also consider how long they have been with the company. Investing with an inexperienced franchiser may be riskier than investing with an experienced one.

Litigation History

The disclosure document helps you assess the background of the franchiser and its executives by requiring the disclosure of prior litigation. The disclosure document tells you if the franchiser or any of its executive officers have been convicted of felonies involving, for example, fraud, any violation of franchise law, unfair or deceptive practices law, or are subject to any state or federal injunctions involving similar misconduct.

It also will tell you if the franchiser or any of its executives have been held liable or settled a civil action involving the franchise relationship. A number of claims against the franchiser may indicate that it has not performed according to its agreements or, at the very least, that franchisees have been dissatisfied with the franchiser's performance. Be aware that some franchisers may try to conceal an executive's litigation history by removing the individual's name from their disclosure documents.

Bankruptcy

The disclosure document tells you if the franchiser or any of its executives have recently

been involved in a bankruptcy. This will help you to assess the franchiser's financial stability and general business acumen, as well as predict if the company is financially capable of delivering promised support services.

Costs

The disclosure document tells you the costs involved to start one of the company's franchises. It will describe any initial deposit or franchise fee, which may be nonrefundable, and costs for initial inventory, signage, equipment, leases, or rentals. Be aware that there may be other undisclosed costs. The following checklist will help you ask about potential costs to you as a franchisee.

- Continuing royalty payments
- Advertising payments, both to local and national advertising funds
- Grand opening or other initial business promotions
- Business or operating licenses
- Product or service supply costs
- Real estate and leasehold improvements
- Discretionary equipment such as a computer system or business alarm system
- Training
- Legal fees
- Financial and accounting advice
- Insurance
- Compliance with local ordinances, such as zoning, waste removal, and fire and other safety codes
- Health insurance
- Employee salaries and benefits

It may take several months or longer to get your business started. Consider in your total cost estimate the operating expenses for the first year and personal living expenses for up to two years. Compare your estimates with what other franchisees have paid and competing franchise systems; perhaps you can get a better deal with another franchiser. An accountant can help you to evaluate this information.

Restrictions

Your franchiser may restrict how you operate your outlet. The disclosure document tells you if the franchiser limits:

- The supplier of goods from whom you may purchase
- The goods or services you may offer for sale

- The customers to whom you can offer goods or services
- The territory in which you can sell goods or services

Understand that restrictions such as these may significantly limit your ability to exercise your own business judgment in operating your outlet.

Terminations

The disclosure document tells you the conditions under which the franchiser may terminate your franchise and your obligations to the franchiser after termination. It also tells you the conditions under which you can renew, sell, or assign your franchise to other parties.

Training and Other Assistance

The disclosure document will explain the franchiser's training and assistance program. Make sure you understand the level of training offered. The following checklist will help you ask the right questions.

- How many employees are eligible for training?
- Can new employees receive training and, if so, is there any additional cost?
- How long are the training sessions?
- How much time is spent on technical training, business management training, and marketing?
- Who teaches the training courses and what are their qualifications?
- What type of ongoing training does the company offer and at what cost?
- Whom can you speak to if problems arise?
- How many support personnel are assigned to your area?
- How many franchisees will the support personnel service?
- Will someone be available to come to your franchised outlet to provide more individual assistance?

The level of training you need depends on your own business experience and knowledge of the franchiser's goods and services. Keep in mind that a primary reason for investing in the franchise, as opposed to starting your own business, is training and assistance. If you have doubts that the training will be sufficient to handle day-to-day business operations, consider another franchise opportunity more suited to your background.

Advertising

You often must contribute a percentage of your income to an advertising fund, even if you disagree with how these funds are used. The disclosure document provides information on advertising costs. The following checklist will help you assess whether the franchiser's advertising will benefit you.

- How much of the advertising fund is spent on administrative costs?
- Are there other expenses paid from the advertising fund?
- Do franchisees have any control over how the advertising dollars are spent?
- What advertising promotions have the company already engaged in?
- What advertising developments are expected in the near future?
- How much of the fund is spent on national advertising?
- How much of the fund is spent on advertising in your area?
- How much of the fund is spent on selling more franchises?
- Do all franchisees contribute equally to the advertising fund?
- Do you need the franchiser's consent to conduct your own advertising?
- Are there rebates or advertising contribution discounts if you conduct your own advertising?
- Does the franchiser receive any commissions or rebates when it places advertisements?
- Do franchisees benefit from such commissions or rebates, or does the franchiser profit from them?

Current and Former Franchisees

The disclosure document provides important information about current and former franchisees. Determine how many franchises are currently operating; a large number of franchisees in your area may mean increased competition. Pay attention to the number of terminated franchisees; a large number of terminated, canceled, or non-renewed franchises may indicate problems.

Be aware that some companies may try to conceal the number of failed franchises by repurchasing failed outlets and then listing them as company-owned outlets. If you buy an existing outlet, ask the franchiser how many owners operated that outlet and over what period of time. A number of different owners over a short period of time may indicate that the location is not a profitable one or that the franchiser has not supported that outlet with promised services.

The disclosure document gives you the names and addresses of current franchisees that have left the system within the last year. Speaking with current and former franchisees is probably the most reliable way to verify the franchiser's claims.

Visit or phone as many of the current and former franchisees as possible; ask them about their experiences. See for yourself the volume and type of business being done.

The following checklist will help you ask current and former franchisees important questions:

- How long has the franchisee operated the franchise?
- Where is the franchise located?
- What was their total investment?
- Were there any hidden or unexpected costs?
- How long did it take them to cover operating costs and earn a reasonable income?
- Are they satisfied with the cost, delivery, and quality of the goods or services sold?
- What were their backgrounds prior to becoming a franchisee?
- Was the franchiser's training adequate?
- What ongoing assistance does the franchiser provide?
- Are they satisfied with the franchiser's advertising program?
- Does the franchiser fulfill its contractual obligations?
- Would the franchisee invest in another outlet?
- Would the franchisee recommend the investment to someone with your goals, income requirements, and background?

Be aware that some franchisers may give you a separate reference list of selected franchisees to contact. Be careful. Those on the list may be individuals who are paid by the franchiser to give a good opinion of the company.

Earnings Potential

You may want to know how much money you can make if you invest in a particular franchise system. Be careful; earnings projections can be misleading. Insist upon written substantiation for any earnings projections or suggestions about your potential income or sales.

Franchisers are not required to make earnings claims, but if they do, the FTC's Franchise Rule requires franchisers to have a reasonable basis for these claims and to provide you with a document that substantiates them. This substantiation includes the bases and assumptions upon which these claims are made. Make sure you get and review the earnings claims document. Consider the following in reviewing any earnings claims.

- *Sample Size.* A franchiser may claim that franchisees in its system earned, for example, $50,000 last year. This claim may be deceptive, however, if only a few franchisees earned that income and it does not represent the typical earnings of franchisees. Ask how many franchisees were included in the number.

- *Average Incomes.* A franchiser may claim that the franchisees in its system earn an average income of, for example, $75,000 a year. Average figures like this tell you very little about how each individual franchisee performs. Remember, a few very successful franchisees can inflate the average. An average figure may make the overall franchise system look more successful than it actually is.

- *Gross Sales.* Some franchisers provide figures for the gross sales revenues of their franchisees. These figures, however, do not tell you anything about the franchisees' actual costs or profits. An outlet with high gross sales revenue on paper actually may be losing money because of high overhead, rent, and other expenses.

- *Net Profits.* Franchisers often do not have data on the net profits of their franchisees. If you do receive net profit statements, ask whether they provide information about company-owned outlets. Company-owned outlets might have lower costs because they can buy equipment, inventory, and other items in larger quantities, or may own, rather than lease, their property.

- *Geographic Relevance.* Earnings may vary in different parts of the country. An ice cream store franchise in a southern state, such as Florida, may expect to earn more income than a similar franchise in a northern state, such as Minnesota. If you hear that a franchisee earned a particular income, ask where that franchisee is located.

- *Franchisee's Background.* Keep in mind that franchisees have varying levels of skills and educational backgrounds. Franchisees with advanced technical or business backgrounds can succeed in instances where more typical franchisees cannot. The success of some franchisees is no guarantee that you will be equally successful.

Financial History

The disclosure document provides you with important information about the company's financial status, including audited financial statements. Be aware that investing in a financially unstable franchiser is a significant risk; the company may go out of business or into bankruptcy after you have invested your money.

Hire a competent franchise attorney or an accountant to review the franchiser's financial statements. Do not attempt to extract this important information from the disclosure document unless you have considerable background in these matters. Your lawyer or accountant can help you understand the following:

- Does the franchiser have steady growth?
- Does the franchiser have a growth plan?
- Does the franchiser make most of its income from the sale of franchises or from continuing royalties?
- Does the franchiser devote sufficient funds to support its franchise system?

Pre-Purchase Research

In addition to the routine investigation that should be conducted prior to any business purchase, potential franchise buyers should be able to contact other franchisees before deciding to invest. They should also obtain a uniform offering circular containing vital details about the franchise's legal, financial, and personnel history before signing a contract.

Reasonable Expectations

Before signing, you should make sure you will have the right to:

- Use the franchise name and trademark
- Receive training and management assistance from the franchiser
- Use the franchiser's expertise in marketing, advertising, facility design, layouts, displays, and fixtures
- Do business in an area protected from other competing franchisees

In some cases, the franchisee may negotiate to have the franchiser help obtain building permits, purchase or lease equipment, signs, and supplies, and construct or remodel the business premises.

Possible Pitfalls

The contract between the two parties usually benefits the franchiser far more than the franchisee. The franchisee is generally subject to meeting sales quotas and is required to purchase equipment, supplies, and inventory exclusively from the franchiser. The franchiser often has the right to terminate the franchise if it fails to operate the business according to the agreement, becomes delinquent on royalties, or violates other contract specifications.

Conclusion

The tax rules surrounding buying a currently operating business or a franchise are often complex, and an attorney, preferably a specialist in business and franchise law, should assist you in evaluating the franchise package and tax considerations. An accountant may be needed to determine the full costs of purchasing and operating the business and to assess the potential profit to the franchisee.

Whether you want to start a brand-new business, buy a currently operating one, or buy a franchise, you should carefully investigate the venture. Performing due diligence in reviewing financial information, past and present owners, and the opportunity as a whole will set you on the High-Performance Entrepreneurial track.

Resources

- **Federal Trade Commission's Franchise and Business Opportunity FAQs**
  www.ftc.gov/bcp/franchise/faq1.htm

- **HiPer Solutions**
  www.hipercoaching.com
  Business coaching from experienced and successful entrepreneurs. Successful training programs on business planning, Web marketing, and leadership development.

- **Service Corps of Retired Executives (SCORE)**
  www.score.org
  Link to retired professionals who are available to give you advice.

- **Small Business Development Centers (SBDC)**
  www.sba.gov/sbdc
  Links to organizations to help your small business grow and prosper.

- **Network of Training and Counseling Services**
  www.sba.gov/ed
  Find free training on business development, business plans, management issues, accounting, funding, and many more.

- **Chambers of Commerce**
  www.uschamber.com

- **Trade Associations**
  www.fita.org

- **SBA's *Is Franchising for Me?* Workbook**
  www.sba.gov

- **Franchise Registry**
  www.franchiseregistry.com

- **Franchise Directories and Evaluation**
  http://sbdcnet.org/SBIC/franchise.php

- **SBA's *Consumer Guide to Buying a Franchise***
  www.sba.gov

- **International Franchise Association**
  www.franchise.org
  The largest membership organization in the world promoting franchising.

- ***Entrepreneur* Magazine's Franchise Zone**
  www.entrepreneur.com/FranchiseZone

[Strategy 4]

The High-Performance Entrepreneur Finances His Venture and Expansion

David P. Hale, PhD

Why not invest your assets in the companies you really like? Like Mae West said,
"To much of a good thing can be wonderful."
Warren Buffet

Every business is different and has its own specific financial needs at different stages of development; therefore, there is no generic method for estimating your startup costs. Some businesses can be started on a shoestring budget, while others may require considerable investment in inventory or equipment. It is vital to know whether you will have enough money to launch your business venture.

To determine your startup costs, you must identify all the expenses your business will incur during its startup phase. Some of these expenses will be one-time expenditures, such as the fee for incorporating your business or the price of a sign for your building. Some expenses will be ongoing, such as the cost of utilities, inventory, insurance, etc. Review your work from strategy 1 for more information.

While identifying these costs, decide whether they are essential or optional. Are they a need or a want? A realistic startup budget should include only those elements necessary to start the business. These essential expenses can then be divided into two separate categories: fixed (overhead) expenses and variable (related to business sales) expenses. Fixed expenses will include figures like the monthly rent, utilities, and administrative and insurance costs. Variable expenses will include inventory, shipping and packaging costs, sales commissions, and other costs associated with the direct sale of a product or service.

The most effective way to calculate your startup costs is to use a worksheet that lists the various categories of costs (both one-time and ongoing) that you will need to estimate prior to starting your business. The following online tools will assist you in performing that task:

- PaloAlto Startup Cost Estimator
  www.bplans.com/common/calculators/startingcosts.cfm
- SBA Small Business Services
  www.sbaonline.sba.gov/

Borrowing Money for Your Business

Borrowing money is one of the most common sources of funding for a small business, but obtaining a loan is not always easy. Before you approach your banker for a loan, it is a good idea to understand as much as you can about the factors the bank will evaluate when they consider making you a loan. This discussion outlines some of the key factors a bank uses to analyze a potential borrower. Also included is a self-assessment checklist at the end of this section for you to complete.

Ask yourself these questions:

How much money do I need to start my business? _____
Who is the best lender for me? _____
What is the lender's minimum and maximum
loan amount? _____
Can the lender meet my current and future
financial needs? _____
Will the lender finance my type of business? _____
Does the lender want collateral? _____

Key Points to Consider

Let's begin by exploring some of the key points your banker will review:

1. Ability to Repay the Loan (Capacity)

The ability to repay must be justified in your loan package. Banks want to see two sources of repayment—cash flow from the business, plus a secondary source such as collateral. In order to analyze the cash flow of the business, the lender will review the business's past financial statements. Generally, banks feel most comfortable dealing with a business that has been in existence for a number of years because they have a financial track record. If the business has consistently made a profit and that profit can cover the payment of additional debt, then it is likely that the loan will be approved. If however, the business has been operating marginally and now has a new opportunity to grow, or if that business is a startup, then it is necessary to prepare a thorough loan package with a detailed explanation addressing how the business will be able to repay the loan.

2. Credit History

One of the first things a bank will determine when a person/business requests a loan is whether their personal and business credit is good. With that in mind, before you go to the bank, or even start the process of preparing a loan request, you want to make sure your credit is good and your credit history is in order.

First, get your personal credit report. You can obtain a report by calling TransUnion (www.transunion.com), Equifax (www.equifax.com), and Experian/ TRW (www.experian.com). By federal law, these three bureaus must provide a free credit report to you once per year. It is important that you initiate this step well in advance of seeking a loan. Personal credit reports may contain errors or be out of date. In many cases, people find that they paid off a bill, but that it was not recorded on their credit report. It can take three to four weeks for this error to be corrected, and it is up to you to see that this happens. You want to make sure that when the bank pulls your credit report, all the errors have been corrected and your history is up-to-date. In addition, if there are credit cards listed that you no longer use, cancel them and have the credit bureaus remove them from your report.

Once you obtain your credit report, how do you know what it says? Many people receive their credit reports, yet have no idea what the strange numbers signify. The following should help in interpreting and checking your personal credit report.

First, check your name, social security number, and address at the top of the page. Make sure these are correct. There are people who have found that they have credit information from another person because of mistakes in their identification information.

On the rest of your credit report, you will see a list of all the credit you have obtained in the past—credit cards, mortgages, student loans, etc. Each credit will be listed individually with information on how you paid that credit off. Any credit you have had a problem paying will be listed toward the top of the list. These credits may affect your ability to obtain a loan.

If you have been late by a month on an occasional payment, this probably will not adversely affect your credit. However, if you are continuously late in paying your credit, have a credit that was never paid and charged off, have a judgment against you, or have declared bankruptcy in the last seven years, it is likely that you will have difficulty obtaining a loan.

In some cases, a person has had a period of bad credit based on a divorce, medical crisis, or some other significant event. If you can show that your credit was good before and after this event and that you have tried to pay back those debts incurred in the period of bad credit, you should be able to obtain a loan. It is best if you write an explanation of your credit problems and how you have rectified them. Attach your written explanation to the credit report you enclose in your loan package.

Each credit bureau has a slightly different way of presenting your credit information. You can get specific information on how to read your credit report from the appropriate company, but here are a few tips to get you started:

Experian

In the last few years, Experian/TRW has prepared credit reports with words and not numbers. Good credits should read "Never Late," "Paid as Agreed."

TransUnion

On the right side of the page on the credit report are number and letter combinations, "I" means installment credit, and "R" means revolving credit. The key information is in the numbers. A "1" means perfect credit since you have always paid your bills on time. A "2" or "3" means you have been two to three months late in paying your bills. Too many of theses will hurt your chances of obtaining credit. A "9" means delinquency in paying your bills and a charge off. This could make it difficult to obtain a loan.

If you need assistance in interpreting or evaluating your credit report, you can ask your accountant or a friendly banker. If your credit report has a few problems on it, you may find that another bank may evaluate your credit report differently.

3. Equity

Financial institutions want to see a certain amount of equity in a business. Equity can be built up in a business through retained earnings or the injection of cash from either the owner or investors. Most banks want to see that the total liabilities or debt of a business is not more than four times the amount of equity. (Stated differently, when you divide total liabilities by equity, your answer should not be more than four.) Therefore, if you want a loan, you must ensure that there is enough equity in the company to leverage that loan. Review your work from strategy 1 for this information.

Do not begin to think that startup businesses can obtain 100 percent financing through conventional or special loan programs. A business owner usually must put some of her/his own money into the business. The amount an individual must put into the business in order to obtain a loan is dependent on the type of loan, purpose, and terms. For example, most banks want the owner to put in at least 20–40 percent of the total requested.

Example: You want $100,000 to start your business. You must put $20,000 of your own money into the new business as equity. Your loan will be $80,000. The debt to equity ratio is 4:1. Note also that this is only one of many factors used to evaluate the business. Just having the right debt/equity ratio does not guarantee you will get the loan.

The balance sheet indicates the amount of equity or net worth of a business. The net worth of the business is often a combination of retained earnings and owner's equity. In many cases, owner's equity will be shown as a loan from shareholders and therefore a liability. If you, as a business owner, wish to obtain a loan, you will be obligated to pay the bank back first and not yourself. Consequently, it may be necessary to restructure the liability so that it becomes owner's equity or subordinate the loan. If your current debt to net worth ratio is 4:1 or over, it is unlikely that you will be able to obtain additional debt/loan.

4. Collateral

Financial institutions are looking for a second source of repayment, which many times means collateral. Collateral are those personal and business assets that can be sold to pay back the loan. Every loan program, even many microloan programs, requires at least some collateral to secure a loan. If a potential borrower has no collateral to secure a loan, s/he will need a co-signer that has collateral to pledge. Otherwise, it may be difficult to obtain a loan.

The value of collateral is not based on the market value. It is discounted to take into account the value that would be lost if the assets had to be liquidated.

The following table gives a general approximation on how different forms of collateral are valued by a typical bank and the SBA:

COLLATERAL TYPE	BANK	SBA
House	Market Value x .75 - Mortgage balance	Market Value x .80 - Mortgage balance
Car	Nothing	Nothing
Truck and Heavy Equipment	Depreciated Value x .50	Same
Office Equipment	Nothing	Nothing
Furniture and Fixtures	Depreciated Value x .50	Same
Inventory: Perishables	Nothing	Nothing

Jewelry	Nothing	Nothing
Other	10%–50%	10%–50%
Receivables	Under 90 days x .75	Under 90 days x .50
Stocks and Bonds	50%–90%	50%–90%
Mutual Funds	Nothing	Nothing
IRA	Nothing	Nothing
CD	100%	100%

Collateral Coverage Ratio

The bank will calculate your collateral coverage ratio as part of the loan evaluation process. This is calculated as follows:

$$\frac{\text{Total Discounted Collateral Value}}{\text{Total Loan Request}} = \text{Collateral Coverage Ratio}$$

5. Experience

A person who wants to open a business and has no experience in that business should not seek financing, let alone start the business unless they intend to hire people or take on a partner who has the appropriate experience. Regardless, the prospective business owner should be advised to take some time to work in the business first and take some entrepreneurial training classes.

The Key Questions the Banker Will be Seeking to Answer Are as Follows:

- Can the business repay the loan? (Is cash flow greater than debt?)
- Can the business owner repay the loan if the business fails? (Is collateral sufficient to repay the loan?)
- Does the business collect its bills?
- Does the business control its inventory?
- Does the business pay its bills?
- Are the officers committed to the business?
- Does the business have a profitable operating history?
- Does the business match its sources and uses of funds?
- Are sales growing?

- Does the business control its expenses?
- Are profits increasing as a percentage of sales?
- Is there any discretionary cash flow?
- What is the future of the industry?
- Who is the competition and what are their strengths and weaknesses?

These items are sometimes classified under what banker's refer to as the eight Cs rule:

- Credit (you must have a good credit rating)
- Capacity to repay the loan
- Capital (are you putting up money of your own)
- Collateral (do you have personal property or other assets)
- Character (are you personable and experienced)
- Conditions (what is the current economic climate and anything that affects your business)
- Commitment (do you have the drive to succeed)
- Cash Flow (will your business profit support the debt and expenses)

Your Banker May Ask:

- How much capital are you investing?
- How will you use the money?
- What terms are you looking for?
- What are you using for collateral?

Do Your Homework First

The best place to start is at the lender's office. Make an appointment with the loan officer and then take the steps listed below. If you are just starting out and know you may have problems obtaining a loan, ask for advice on how to best correct your situation. What better way to allow the lender to know how serious you are than being upfront. Use this opportunity to ask for pointers in writing a business plan to their liking.

- Ask what the lender's criteria are for business loans.
- Ask if the lender will approve your size loan.
- Obtain a loan application from the lender and study it.

- Make an appointment. Do not show up unannounced.
- You are being interviewed. Ensure you have practiced your presentation several times. Even if you are on a fact-finding interview, be professionally dressed and act as if you are actually asking for a loan.
- You are selling yourself and your business. Be on your A-game. You must persuade the lender that you are worthy.

Game Plan When Meeting the Lender

- Have several copies of your business plan, the completed loan application, and anything else you will need.
- Your presentation should not be longer than thirty minutes. It is preferred that you offer an outline at the beginning. Your ending is as important as the beginning.
- Offer your lender a tour of your business operation or facility.
- Ensure you can back up anything you say.
- Determine how long it will take to obtain an answer.
- After leaving the meeting, send the lender a thank-you note and possibly make a thank-you phone call.

SBA Loan Programs

The SBA offers numerous loan programs to assist small businesses. It is important to note, however, that the SBA is primarily a guarantor of loans made by private and other institutions and does not offer loans to small businesses. We will review the more commonly used SBA loan programs:

- Basic 7(a) Loan Program
- Pre-qualification Program
- CDC/504 Program
- Micro-Loans
- Patriot Loan Program

Basic 7(a) Loan Guaranty

The Basic 7(a) Loan Guaranty serves as the SBA's primary business loan program to help qualified small businesses obtain financing when they might not be eligible for business loans through normal lending channels. It is also the agency's most flexible business loan program, since financing under this program can be guaranteed for a variety of general business purposes.

Loan proceeds can be used for most sound business purposes including working capital, machinery and equipment, furniture and fixtures, land and building (including purchase, renovation, and new construction), leasehold improvements, and debt refinancing (under special conditions). Loan maturity is up to ten years for working capital and generally up to twenty-five years for fixed assets. SBA offers multiple variations of the basic 7(a) loan program to accommodate targeted needs.

Who qualifies? Startup and existing small businesses, commercial lending institutions.

Who is the program delivered through? Most commercial lending institutions.

SBA Loan Pre-qualification

Pre-qualification allows business applicants to have their loan applications for $250,000 or less analyzed and potentially sanctioned by the SBA before they are taken to lenders for consideration. The program focuses on the applicant's character, credit, experience, and reliability rather than assets. An SBA-designated intermediary works with the business owner to review and strengthen the loan application. The review is based on key financial ratios, credit and business history, and the loan-request terms. The program is administered by the SBA's Office of Field Operations and SBA district offices.

This operates much like obtaining a pre-qualification for a home mortgage. If this is your first time obtaining a business loan, this may be your best bet. The more prepared you are going into a lender to seek funding, the better your chances will be in securing a loan.

Who qualifies? Any small businesses.

Who is the program delivered through? Intermediaries operating in specific geographic areas. The Loan Pre-qualification Program uses intermediary organizations to assist prospective borrowers in developing viable loan application packages and securing loans. This program targets low-income borrowers, disabled business owners, new and emerging businesses, veterans, exporters, rural and specialized industries.

The job of the intermediary is to work with the applicant to make sure the business owner's business plan is complete and that the application is both eligible and has credit merit. If the intermediary is satisfied that the application has a chance for approval, the intermediary will send it to the SBA for processing. To find out whether there is a pre-qualification intermediary operating in your area, contact your local SBA office.

{Note:} Small Business Development Centers serving as intermediaries do not charge a fee for loan packaging. Put simply, they do it for free. For qualified entrepreneurs operating on a shoestring budget and bootstrapping their business venture, this is your ticket. For-profit organizations will charge a fee.

Once the loan package is completed, it is submitted to the SBA for expedited consideration. SBA conducts a thorough analysis of the case, using the same period of time and degree of analysis that it uses when processing requests under the regular method of delivery process.

If the SBA decides the application is eligible and has sufficient credit merit to warrant approval, it will issue a commitment letter on behalf of the applicant. The commitment letter or pre-qualification letter indicates SBA's willingness to guaranty a loan made by a lender under certain terms and conditions. The intermediary then helps the borrower locate a lender offering the most competitive rates. The applicant then takes the letter and its application documents to a lender for a decision.

Certified Development Company (CDC), A 504 Loan Program

This program provides long-term, fixed-rate financing to small businesses to acquire real estate or machinery or equipment for expansion or modernization. Typically, a 504 project includes a loan secured from a private-sector lender with a senior lien, a loan secured from a CDC (funded by a 100 percent SBA-guaranteed debenture) with a junior lien covering up to 40 percent of the total cost, and a contribution of at least 10 percent equity from the borrower.

Who qualifies? Any small business requiring "brick and mortar" financing.

Who is the program delivered through? Certified development companies (private, nonprofit corporations set up to contribute to the economic development of their communities or regions).

Microloan, A 7(m) Loan Program

The microloan program provides short-term loans of up to $35,000 to small businesses and not-for-profit child-care centers for working capital or the purchase of inventory, supplies, furniture, fixtures, machinery and/or equipment. Proceeds cannot be used to pay existing debts or to purchase real estate. The SBA makes or guarantees a loan to an intermediary, who in turn, makes the microloan to the applicant. These organizations also provide management and technical assistance. The loans are not guaranteed by the SBA. The microloan program is available in selected locations in most states.

Who qualifies? Small businesses and not-for-profit child-care centers needing small-scale financing and technical assistance for startup or expansion.

Who is the program delivered through? Specially designated intermediary lenders (nonprofit organizations with experience in lending and in technical assistance).

Patriot Express Loan Program

The new Patriot Express loan is offered by the SBA network of participating lenders nationwide and features fast turnaround time for loan approvals. Loans are available up to $500,000 and qualify for SBA's maximum guaranty of up to 85 percent for loans of $150,000 or less, and up to 75 percent for loans over $150,000 up to $500,000. For loans above $350,000, lenders are required to take all available collateral.

The Patriot Express loan can be used for most business and franchise purposes, including startup, expansion, equipment purchases, working capital, inventory, or business-occupied real-estate purchases.

Patriot Express loans feature SBA's lowest interest rates for business loans, generally 2.25 percent to 4.75 percent over the prime lending rate depending upon the size and maturity of the loan. Your local SBA district office will have a listing of Patriot Express lenders in your area.

How to Prepare a Loan Package

Finding financing to start and expand a company is an age-old problem, and most entrepreneurs find it to be one of the greatest struggles they face. While the process can be time-consuming, frustrating, and intimidating, if you are informed and well prepared, your chances of securing the needed capital are greatly increased.

In putting together a loan package, ask yourself the following basic questions. The answers to them and the information provided to back them up are essential to the lending decision and its speed.

1. What is the specific purpose of the loan? Your lender or investor will review your financial requirements among three types of capital acquisition:

- *Working Capital:* Used to meet fluctuating needs that will be repaid during the company's next full operating cycle, generally one year.
- *Growth Capital:* Used to meet needs that will be repaid with profits over a several-year period (usually not more than seven years). If seeking growth capital, you will be expected to show how the money will be used to increase profits sufficiently to repay the loan in the agreed-upon time frame.
- *Equity Capital:* Used to meet permanent needs. Equity capital must be raised from investors who will take a risk in return for some combination of dividend returns, capital gains, or a specific share of the business.

2. What amount of financing will support my needs? Do not ask, how much can I borrow? Have enough existing capital so that, augmented by the loan, the business can operate on a sound financial basis. For new businesses, this includes sufficient resources to withstand startup expenses and the initial operating phase, during which losses are likely to occur. Be able to inject between one third and one-half of the total capital required. If you plan to borrow equity from friends or relatives, determine what the repayment terms will be.

3. When and for how long will I need these funds? Most of today's lenders are providing growth capital in the form of asset-based loans (i.e., loans for acquiring land, buildings, or equipment that can be used as security). While the majority of these loans carry terms of three to seven years, some may extend over longer periods. For financial planning purposes, the entrepreneur should keep in mind that longer loan periods incur larger overall interest costs.

4. How will I generate sufficient cash flow to repay the loan? Consider the situation from the lender's point of view: if you were asked to lend someone money, you'd want assurance of being paid back in full, and in a timely manner.

5. What collateral can be utilized (if applicable)? Estimate its value, and be ready to provide supporting appraisals.

6. Will the owners provide personal guarantees? Having a comprehensive and well thought-out business plan is essential in obtaining financing. In fact, without one, even stepping into the bank is pointless. To lenders or potential investors, a plan not only provides information and reveals your evaluation of your venture's feasibility, but also reflects your management abilities. An analytical, objective business plan convinces lenders you are cautious, conservative, and capable. One that is poorly researched, makes unsupported assumptions, or draws unfounded conclusions shows you are inexperienced and—in their eyes—reckless. Lenders receive so many proposals that they cannot afford to spend much time evaluating each business plan. That means your plan has only a few minutes to make a good impression, and must therefore speak for itself as a sales tool. One key is to make sure your business plan is as thorough and accurate as possible and that you can back up all your claims with facts.

Business Plan

Your business plan should include:

- **Executive Summary**
  This portion concisely summarizes the key elements of the business plan that follow, and should convince the lender that it is worthwhile to review the plan in detail. Include information about the loan being sought in terms of amount, purpose, duration, and how you intend to pay it back.

- **Company History/Organization/Management**
  Describe the historical development of the business, including legal form of organization, significant changes, subsidiaries, degree of ownership, and the principals' roles they played in the firm's foundation. Detail their experience and the management and decision-making structure. Also include an organizational chart and discuss other key personnel and their responsibilities.

- **Product/Service**
  Detail the present or planned product or service lines, including their relative importance (with sales projections, if possible), evaluation (use, quality, performance), competitive advantage, and demand.

- **Market Analysis/Marketing Strategy**
  You should be able to estimate how many customers you will have and how near they are to your location, as well as their age, family structure, lifestyle, disposable income, and purchasing habits. Explain why your product/service is desirable to them, the scope of your firm's marketing and selling activities (including pricing policy), and what share of the market you will realistically be able to capture based on the industry analysis that follows.

- **Industry Analysis (Competition)**
  It is equally important to know about your field and have a keen sense of the competition. List your major competitors by name and describe how

closely located they are, what products/services they provide, what they do better/worse, and how profitable/successful they are. Also, elaborate on the industry itself, including an industry outlook, principal markets, industry size, and major characteristics. Describe the effects of any major social, economic, technological, or regulatory trends.

- **Production/Operating Plan**
  Explain how the firm will perform production or delivery of service in terms of physical facilities, suppliers, labor supply (current and planned), technologies/skills required, manufacturing process (if applicable), and cost breakdown for materials, labor, and overhead.

According to the SBA, the following items will also be needed to support a loan request:

- **Sources and Uses of Funds Statement**
  The potential lender will require a statement of how you intend to disperse the loan funds; back up your statement with supporting data. For example, buying a commercial building will require a preliminary title report, an appraisal, an escrow, and title insurance, among other documents.

- **Cash Flow Statement (Budget)**
  These documents (used for internal planning) project what your business means in terms of dollars and show cash inflow and outflow over a period of time. If you've been in business for some time, worksheets can be compiled from the actual figures of income and expenses in previous years combined with projected changes for the next period. If starting a new business, you will have to project your financial needs and disbursements.

- **Three-Year Income Projection**
  This pro-forma projection only includes income and deductible expenses, while the cash flow statement (above) includes all sources of cash and monies to be paid out. Find out the lender's specific requirements as to whether income and expenses should be projected on an annual or monthly basis.

- **Breakeven Analysis**
  The breakeven point is the point at which a company's expenses exactly match its sales or service volume, and the firm neither makes a profit nor incurs a loss. It can be calculated in either mathematical or graph form and expressed in total dollars or revenue exactly offset by total expenses.

- **Balance Sheet**

  This financial statement, usually prepared at the close of an accounting period, shows the financial condition of the business as of a fixed date. By regularly preparing it, you will be able to identify and analyze trends in the financial strength of your firm and thus implement timely modifications.

- **Income Statement**

  In contrast to the balance sheet, this statement shows what has happened to your business over a period of time; it is an excellent tool for assessing your business. It enables you to identify weaknesses in your operation (such as the timing of an advertising campaign that did not increase sales as anticipated) and devise more effective ways to run your company and thereby increase profits. Similarly, you might examine your income statement to see which months have the heaviest sales volume and plan inventory accordingly. Comparison of income statements from several years will provide an excellent picture of the trends in your business.

As a sole proprietor or principal of a corporation, you may be asked to back up your business loan with personal assets (your house, stocks, or bonds). If you are in a partnership, a personal guarantee must be signed by all principals for repayment of the loan.

It is important to emphasize that businesses with several years of successful operation will find it far easier to obtain financing than startups, as lenders will be much more receptive and confident in your ability to repay a loan at that point. In fact, without a strong business plan with realistic expectations and forecasts, managerial experience, and collateral, it may be impossible for a new business to get a loan at all. Lenders are always leery of extending financing to new ventures or unproven management teams, as they represent a high risk of default.

This doesn't mean you can't get a loan as a startup, but rather that you will have to compensate for the lack of a track record by being strong and well prepared in other areas. Demonstrate by your enthusiasm and the thoroughness of your business plan that you are committed to the venture and that it will succeed. After all, when applying for a loan, you're selling both yourself and your business.

How Banks Evaluate Loan Requests

In putting together the best possible package to secure a business loan, it's important to know what happens after you leave the bank and the lending officer evaluates your request.

An advantage of preparing an effectively organized loan application (including the all-important business plan) is that it will significantly decrease the time spent waiting for an answer. Many bankers have found that in about 80 percent of the cases, the formal loan request is not complete. Much of the time spent in approving a loan can be traced to the banker having to ask the potential borrower for more information or for clarification of the information that has already been submitted.

In evaluating loan applications, banks use the three Cs of credit—character, capacity, and collateral.

1. Character. Character is actually a check on your financial status and personal credit history, including your previous loan payment record. The theory is that people are creatures of habit—if you have repaid a loan on time before, you will repay this one as well. Conversely, if you have defaulted on a previous loan, the danger is that you will tend to default again.

Also considered is experience in the type of business you are trying to finance, including level of responsibility, education, and business management training. Lenders are particularly concerned that potential borrowers have a solid understanding of financial record keeping, business credit, the importance of collecting accounts receivable, inventory control and turnover, and marketing their product or service.

If your prior business experience is not relevant to your current venture (for example, if your career has been in the corporate world, and you want to start a restaurant), banks will be leery about your ability to run the new endeavor successfully and thus repay the loan.

2. Capacity. Prudent bankers have always looked first to the cash flow of the business as the way the loan will be repaid, which underlines the importance of preparing a cash flow statement with future cash flow projections before presenting your loan request. Doing so indicates to the lender that you are knowledgeable about the cash coming into your business, and are therefore better able to avoid a cash shortage that would jeopardize making monthly payments.

3. Collateral. While cash flow is the primary source of loan repayment, lenders will want a backup or secondary source as an exit or last resort, should your business not prove profitable. Collateral—defined as "anything of value used as security for repayment of a debt or performance of a contract"—can be real estate, stocks and bonds, savings accounts, equipment, accounts receivable, or the cash value of life insurance policies.

Psychologically, lenders feel that borrowers have more interest in repaying the loan if they know that failure to do so will result in the lender taking possession of whatever has been put up for collateral. A lender will also try to obtain personal guarantees so that if you default on the loan, the institution has access to your personal assets.

It is important to note that these days, in the wake of severe economic downturns such as that experienced in the Southwest in the mid-1980s, collateral doesn't carry the weight it used to. Therefore, banks are likely to require more collateral than was previously the case, and evaluate it based on market—rather than replacement—value. Companies without enough collateral to pledge will have to scale back their borrowing needs and make do with less.

One final tip is not to forget "relationship banking." Once a relationship has been established and you've explained your business operations and anticipated needs, it becomes far easier to approach a banker when a loan is needed. This familiarity will make you more credible than a customer who has not taken the time to introduce himself.

Be sure to stay close to your banker. Be open and honest about major changes and significant events, whether good or bad. As your lending officer has to tell your story to other people in the organization (including his superiors), nothing can jinx the relationship faster than a lack of candor. Feeding bankers regular information is, of course, time-consuming when you have a company to run. However, it is all part of building credibility and trust, and will enable you to use your banker's knowledge to help ensure the continued success of your business.

Never Take No for an Answer

Does this sound familiar? You applied for a loan and the bank officer responded with the dreaded words, "I'm sorry, but …" and turned it down. Admittedly an unhappy scenario, it is not a unique one and happens to many businesses at some point.

Fortunately, you can turn what would otherwise be a negative rejection into a positive learning experience by taking steps to find out why the final answer was "no."

Personalize the Process

It helps to first become familiar with how banks actually process loan requests. If special circumstances apply to your business, describe them to the loan officer and ask what additional information might be presented to help your case. Openness about the particulars of your financial situation can help bankers look past the impersonal statistics.

If anomalies exist in your business or credit history, point out and explain them before making the credit application. This personalizes the entire process and helps to establish trust between you and the bank officer and business. It is commonly said that bankers don't like surprises, and one of the worst surprises is discovering bad credit.

Why Didn't I Get the Loan?

Banks most often deny credit because a business has:

- *Bad credit.* As noted above, a clean credit record is crucial in both business and personal finances. Anything else sends the bank warning signals about your likeliness of repaying the loan in a timely fashion—or at all.

- *High debt-to-equity ratio.* A typical ratio is three-to-one. Banks also look at other standard ratios for credit worthiness. In special circumstances, businesses that do not meet the usual standards may still be considered.

- *Insufficient collateral.* This is common for startup businesses that lack collateral or significant assets to pay back the loan if the company should experience hard times.

Other reasons may also lead the bank to reject a loan application. If yours is turned down, it behooves you to find out why the loan officer thought the proposition was too risky. The bank may even have suggestions on how to make your presentation more persuasive. The key is, *ask!*

What Banks and the Government Are Doing

Banks acknowledge the difficulty in getting credit, especially for small, startup, and special sector businesses. Through new programs, government loan guarantees, and private initiatives, however, banks are beginning to increase their loans to these segments. Under the Community Reinvestment Act of 1977, for example, the government began asking banks to make credit more available to small business owners in their own communities. Due to recent government pressure to take action under this act, some banks have developed programs specifically tailored to the needs of small enterprises.

Beyond Banks for Funds

Commercial banks or savings and loan institutions are not the only source of credit. Other sources sometimes take on riskier propositions, albeit at a higher interest rate and possibly with a stake in the company. They may also be able to offer more flexible payback arrangements or alternative revolving loans that regular banks cannot.

Commercial finance companies typically offer revolving loans with a credit line based on accounts receivable and inventory. This is a flexible loan that allows the borrower to repay or borrow money daily, depending on the company's cash flow needs. Interest rates are usually 1 to 4 percent higher than on bank loans, but because the borrower can pay the loan as soon as a payment is received, interest is only charged on money actually used.

Evolving from a past reputation for granting only conservative loans, insurance companies have now moved into all areas of lending, except short-term revolving debt. Most frequently they offer seven- to fifteen-year loans at an interest rate based on the Treasury rate plus a risk premium. Many insurance companies are also interested in buying into growing firms to offset inflation worries on their fixed-return investments.

Venture capital firms may be able to provide growth money for companies in a period of expansion. Although traditionally focused on larger enterprises, venture capital firms have been increasingly willing to finance smaller startup companies. Some firms require voting control before agreeing to finance a company, and most prefer to deal in equity securities or subordinated debt that is convertible to equity.

Whether you are applying for a microloan, SBA guaranteed loan, or a traditional bank loan, similar information is required to complete a loan package. The following checklist provides you with the most common requirements for a loan package.

Loan Checklist

Completed

Personal Financial Information:	
Personal Financial Statements *(signed and dated)*	
Copies of Personal Tax Returns *(including all schedules for three years)*	
Source/Amount of owner's capital injection	
Credit Report for owners of 20 percent or more *(dated within ninety days, with derogatories explained)*	
Resumes from principals, partners, or proprietors	

Financial/Business Information:	
Business Plan	
Description/History of the business	
Benefits from the loan	
Articles of Incorporation or Assumed Name Certificate	
Credit Report for the business and owners of 20 percent or more *(dated within ninety days, with all derogatories explained)*	
Cash Flow Projections *(monthly for one year; second and third years may be quarterly)*	
Projected Profit and Loss *(monthly for one year; second and third years may be quarterly)*	
Notes to Financial Projections *(assumptions)*	
Balance Sheet and Profit and Loss Statement *(for the interim period dated within ninety days, each page signed/dated; startups should include opening balance)*	
Balance Sheet and Profit and Loss Statement *(for last three years, each signed and dated)*	
Copies of Business Income Tax Returns *(for three years)*	
Copy of Existing Facility Lease (s)and/or Lease(s) to be acquired	
Schedule of All Business Term Debt *(notes, contract, and leases payable)*	
Aged Accounts Receivable	
Aged Accounts Payable	
Collateral Requirements:	
Schedule of Fixed Assets to be acquired with loan and their cost	
Appraisal on real estate and most recent Tax Appraisal	
Franchise:	
Franchise Agreement and FTC Disclosure Report*	
Construction, Including Leasehold Improvements:	
Construction Contract* by the contractor, architect, or other, with "turn-key" firm cost quote	
Copy of performance bond*	
Additional Information:	
Partnership Agreements*	
Employment Agreements*	

Change of Ownership/Business Acquisition* *(copy of buy-sell agreement and copy of escrow instructions)*	
Real Estate Acquisition* *(copy of sale/purchase agreement, signed/dated; copy of escrow instructions, to include legal description.)*	
Hazardous Waste Assessments Report(s)*—*(phase one or two, must have for existing gas stations and frequently polluting industries)*	
Real Estate Refinancing or Debt Payment*—*(copies of notes, settlement sheet.)*	
*If applicable	

Conclusion

Unless you are starting your entrepreneurial venture with a sizeable, personal nest egg, at some point you will need to consider outside financial sources. The SBA has business loan programs that fit any size entrepreneurial endeavor. Researching all of your loan options or other sources of financing will assist in supercharging any startup or expansion project.

Lastly, meeting with a prospective banker will provide you with valuable information on how to properly develop a loan application and business plan focused on the bank's requirements. Developing a personal relationship with your banker will additionally serve as a stage for you to project your entrepreneurial passion. This will cement you in the banker's mind as a good risk and a High-Performance Entrepreneur!

[Strategy 5]

The High-Performance Entrepreneur Opens an Office

Timothy P. Maxwell II

No real estate is permanently valuable but the grave.
Mark Twain

By now, your creative juices are flowing. You know what your business goals are, you know what kind of business you want, and you know how to operate your business. You have a plan that will provide you with fulfillment, purpose, and a nice paycheck! You are ready to be your own boss. However, where are you going to do all of these wonderful things? The answer is, in your very own business location! Your location is one of the most important aspects of operating any business, and thus requires you to do some homework.

You have several options when considering where to locate your business. I have categorized the vast number of places you can operate from into three broad locations: your home, a commercial/retail building, or the Internet.

Working at Home

I work at home and I love it! Working at home can be the most wonderful thing. You have no boss, you can go to work in your pajamas, you set your own hours, and you can write off many personal items as business expenses, not to mention you can give yourself raises whenever you want! However, working at home is also very tedious and requires a great deal of organization and motivation. I can't count the amount of times I've awaken to my blaring alarm and considered not even getting up! Every hour is precious, especially when you work at home; you need to maximize your day in order to maintain and increase profits. When you work at home, you have four main things to consider: scheduling, covenants, distractions, and taxes.

Scheduling

Keeping a schedule is often the most difficult thing to do when you work at home because your schedule dictates your day and can change unexpectedly. It is very hard to maintain a consistent schedule, but if you can, it will be very beneficial to you and save you so much stress and money.

Key: Be as prepared as possible for schedule conflicts. Be prepared to think quickly on a daily basis.

Covenants and Zoning

Where you live is most likely zoned residential and thus you will never be able to operate a retail business out of your home. This would cause too much traffic and you would not have enough parking to accommodate customers. More specifically, neighborhoods typically have covenants that outline what is acceptable or unacceptable in that neighborhood. In a condominium or apartment, your lease and your property management regime will have rules outlined that are designed to prevent conflict and damages. According to George McGregor, City-County Planning Director of the Sumter, South Carolina, City-County Planning Commission:

> "The key is to understand the scope of your business. Most zoning will allow you to operate a small computer consulting business out of your attic. But once it rises to the threshold of larger square footage, or you are getting visitors or clients or customers to your house, most zoning ordinances are going to prohibit that and, therefore, your only option is going to be to find space, lease space or own space in a commercial zoning district."

Different neighborhoods have different covenants, and you need to know what they are, even if you do not own and operate a business. Ask questions if you do not know!

Distractions

Being at home can offer many distractions that you would not find if you worked in the office place or outside your home. There are plenty of distractions that can occupy your precious business time, such as laundry, pets, kids, neighbors, and television. If you take a break from something, that break can easily turn into a day off if you allow yourself to become distracted. Minimizing distractions is another task that you have in addition to operating your business. Spanish navigator and adventurer Christopher Columbus said, "By prevailing over all obstacles and distractions, one may unfailingly arrive at his chosen goal or destination." If you want to reach your goals and be successful, you have to prevent, avoid, and overcome distractions.

Taxes

Working at home offers you certain tax benefits and considerations. I am neither a lawyer nor an accountant, so I recommend you contact both types of professionals when considering this aspect of your business. I can, however, tell you what I know: *almost everything is deductible!*

When you work out of your home, almost everything is deductible. You can write off various expenses you incur doing business on your personal taxes that will offset income. A percentage of your home's mortgage, rent, insurance, and taxes can be written off if parts of your home are used to conduct business. If you use a vehicle to conduct business, gas, maintenance, insurance, depreciation, and taxes on that vehicle are tax deductible. If you use your vehicle mostly for business, you will have significant tax write-offs.

Items such as envelopes, paper, stamps, and other office supplies and furniture can also be written off. If you meet clients for lunch or dinner, some of the expenses incurred on those occasions can be written off your taxes. Just make sure that you keep business and personal expenses separated. In deciding which is which, it is a good idea to seek the advice of an accountant or tax specialist. There are also tax traps that you can fall into. See the resource guide at the end of the chapter for further information.

The benefits of working at home are many, and if you can manage your time well and you are motivated and ready for success, then you are well on your way to being a profitable, home-based business owner. If you operate at home for a few years and your business begins to grow exponentially, you may find that you have a need for a physical location away from home. You may also be in the position to expand your services and product offerings. If you are currently at this stage, congratulations!

Commercial or Retail Location

Once your company begins to grow, you may need to expand to accommodate a growing number of products, inventory, and customers. Depending on what type of business you have, you will want to move into a commercial, retail, agricultural, or industrial location.

We won't go too much into agriculture and industry, but if you have an interest in either of these areas, there are references listed in the resource guide at the end of the chapter, and you can always enlist the services of a real estate professional that specializes in your area of interest. When you consider having a commercial/retail location, the three most important areas to pay attention to are exposure, zoning, and deciding if it is better to lease or buy.

Decent Exposure

People will not come into your store or office if they cannot find it. If you are operating a retail business selling clothes, food, or some other product, you may want to be located in a major shopping area within your town. Locating in a high-traffic area exposes your business to thousands of people without ever having to advertise.

If you are starting a medical practice or law office, you will want to locate in an area off the main strip, but still close to shopping and residences. Also, when considering where you want to have your physical location, be cognizant of things such as traffic lights and medians.

If a potential customer cannot make a left-hand turn into your establishment because of a median or an unprotected left light signal, you may lose some customer traffic. Make your location as easy to get in and out of as possible.

Zoning

Zoning is used by cities to separate unwanted uses from each other, to protect property values, and to group land uses into categorical purposes that will benefit the public good. Most zoning laws are location specific, so they will vary from state to state, county to county, and city to city. All zoning ordinances are public information and are accessible at your local county or city courthouse.

Within commercial zoning ordinances, there are sub-categories that further dictate what businesses can be located within the zoned area. Zoning, specifically in commercial areas, is generally based on use. There is a general commercial use, which allows any kind of business to operate in that zone. There could also be a commercial zone just for professionals (e.g., doctors and lawyers), so a car-care center or nail salon would not be able to operate in that area.

Say you purchase a store on the main strip in a C-1 zone and you want to open a bar. If C-1 is a zone that does not allow alcohol or the neighboring businesses do not want you to sell alcohol, you cannot locate your bar there. Having said that, you may be able to get your building rezoned or request an ordinance so you can locate your business there.

Typically, it is a three-to-six-month process to get a location rezoned. The ordinance will be brought in front of the city and county planning commission, and then must be voted on. The commission members will base their votes on how the public, especially neighboring businesses, respond to the rezoning and how the rezoning will coincide with the city's comprehensive plan. You will have to talk to your county or city planning commissioner to get more details on feasibility.

If you plan to build a commercial or retail location, you will have to obtain building permits and pay for a soil percolation test, often called a "perk," in order to build on the land and to have it zoned in your favor. Getting your land perked, in a nutshell, is just determining the ability of the soil to absorb liquids from your septic system. If the property is zoned correctly and your building is conducive to the city's master plan, you will receive your building permit.

Most areas use what is called Euclidean zoning, which sets strict separation of uses. In other areas of the country, sometimes considered progressive, there are mixed-use developments that combine retail, residential, and commercial buildings in the same area. This allows residents to conveniently walk to a grocery store or doctor's appointment, sometimes not even having to leave the building their home is in.

Leasing Versus Buying

This is probably the biggest decision you will make concerning your business once you decide you want to operate from a commercial or retail location. There are many advantages to both; your decision will be dependent on the type of business you run and the real estate market. The goals of your business, the level of competition, and your potential for growth also influence your lease-versus-buy decision. There are several computer programs (on the resource list) you can buy that will analyze your data and then calculate which choice is better for you financially.

If you buy, you will be the owner. If you lease, then a leasor, or owner, will lease the building to you, the lessee. As the owner, you are responsible for every cost associated with that building. With leasing, you will typically either have a gross lease or a triple net lease.

A gross lease is simply where the tenant pays one large rent amount to the owner, who is responsible for paying taxes, insurance, and maintenance out of that rent.

In a triple net lease, the tenant is responsible for paying the taxes, insurance, and maintenance, in addition to rent to the owner. So how do you know whether to buy or lease?

I recall my days at the University of South Carolina Darla Moore School of Business, where my professor, a local executive at CB Richard Ellis, poured insightful information into us about the "real world" of commercial real estate. Some things I learned were:

When Should You Buy?

- You plan to own and operate your business for many years without changing operations.

- You can find a great location where the land will appreciate.

- The real estate market is moderate or slow, and sellers will sell at decent or lower prices.

- You can purchase a multi-unit building. You will occupy one unit and have your tenants in the other units pay your mortgage!

When Should You Lease?

- When you do not have enough money to buy and/or no money in reserves.

- If your business goals are to expand very rapidly or change operations quickly.

- To test the idea of moving into a commercial location.

- If it is more cost-effective to lease based on return of investment (ROI).

Certain businesses require you to modify your building, and as a lessee, your leasor usually will not allow you to do that. If you operate a business that does not fit the structural needs of current buildings for sale or lease, it may be better to purchase land and build. There are also some firms that own land and will build to suit, which means they will construct whatever building you want and lease it to you, of course in terms favorable to them, but beneficial for you. Make sure you have a lawyer read the contract first to help you make your decision. Now you know *when* you should buy versus lease, but *why* should you buy versus lease?

Advantages of Buying

- You own the building (write off depreciation on taxes).

- You can modify the building as necessary.

- The land will appreciate and you can sell for more than you paid later.
- You have the right to become a leasor and rent it to lessees.

Advantages of Leasing
- There are no maintenance, taxes, or insurance issues to worry about (unless you are on a triple net lease).
- You can move to a new location without having to worry about paying for two locations.
- Less upfront costs and no back end costs.

Donald Trump said, "Sometimes, your best investments are the ones you don't make." This is very true when it comes to purchasing a commercial office or retail building. There are many reasons not to purchase your own space and lease instead. However, on the flipside, there are many reasons to purchase and not lease. It depends on your situation and your needs. Whichever fits your goals, does not hinder your potential, and is more cost-effective in the long term will be your best bet. Remember to do your research and talk with anyone who may know about local laws and trends so that you can make the best decision for your business.

Internet

I am no e-commerce analyst, but I would say you have a wonderful business when hundreds of customers at once can find your business, buy your service or product, and pay you for it—without you even being directly involved in the sale!

Purchases from Internet wholesalers allow you to order your goods online and then resell them through the same venue. You never have to leave your home to buy or sell goods! You could conduct business from a coffee shop. All you need is a computer with an Internet connection. Online stores and Internet businesses are profitable if run right, and in spite of the dot-com fiasco, there are still hundreds of new businesses opening up online daily.

The Internet is such an effective tool because it does not discriminate based on location, like a physical building would. As long as you have a user-friendly Web site that is easy to navigate, you can do business online. The Internet is twenty-four hours a day, seven days a week, so your store will never close, even after you go to sleep. Resources such as eBay and Amazon allow sellers to operate online stores and utilize their search engines to attract customers.

It is easier than ever to open up an online store now that there are businesses to build and maintain your Web site and software to dumb-down HTML and other confusing Internet jargon. This being the case, many businesses are opening up online, thus creating massive competition. If you ever go to www.amazon.com and look at an item, there are generally anywhere between twenty and two hundred sellers of that same item!

American writer and humorist Dave Barry quips, "The Internet is the most important single development in the history of human communication since the invention of call waiting."

Many people are visual learners, so I have compiled everything from this chapter into a graphical format that is easy to read and easy to refer back to in the future. I hope your business is prosperous, and to quote *The Greatest Salesman in the World* by Og Mandino, "The slaughterhouse of failure is not my destiny. I will persist until I succeed."

Comparison of Different Business Locations

	No Location	Home	Office	Internet
Operations	All business is conducted at customer's location.. Only need to consider storage and equipment antennae.	Typically long hours. Lots of computer work, faxes, and e-mails.	Maintain store hours. Hire employees. Need security.	Most operations can be automated and you will be alerted only for important things.
Zoning	Not affected.	Residential zoning. Restricted by neighborhood covenants/homeowner's association.	Commercial/Retail/Industrial/Agricultural zoning. Very specific restrictions about operations and location.	Governed by U.S. e-commerce laws and guidelines.
Lease vs. Buy	*Equipment only:* Typically it is a better investment to buy your equipment, but initially you may need to lease until you can afford it.	Home ownership is the key to wealth; initially, you may lease until you can afford a home.	Based on cost-effectiveness and highest return on investment.	You can't buy the Internet! You have to lease.

Taxes	No property tax or sales tax. Can file taxes on personal or business.	Can file taxes on personal or business.	Must file taxes on business.	State sales tax, shipping and handling, plus taxes if you sell products. Can file taxes on personal or business.
Pros	Most personal expenses are tax deductible. No building to keep up.	Most personal expenses are tax deductible. You set your own hours and don't need employees.	Have a physical location for customers. Have identifiable business in the community.	Most personal expenses are tax deductible. Can work from anywhere. Millions of people can access your store at once.
Cons	Customers have no location to identify with.	Business and home life can be intertwined. Many distractions. Cannot operate a retail business.	Have building maintenance, expenses, security, etc.	No human interaction. A lot of competition.

Conclusion

Depending on what type of business you are operating and it's needs, will dictate where you will be operating from. Checking with your local zoning commission will provide you with the proper rules and laws regarding where to operate from.

If your desire is to open a storefront operation, deciding whether to buy, lease, or rent is a big decision. Make sure you closely review all of the documentation you sign to ensure that you know what responsibilities you have.

It is always a good safeguard to have your attorney review all contracts before signing them. Knowing that you are running your business from a location legally will provide you with a feeling of safety and move you further up the ladder as a High-Performance Entrepreneur!

Resources

E-Commerce

- Internet portal to laws, news, and updates in the field of e-commerce: www.ibls.com/
- *Multiple Streams of internet Income* by Robert G. Allen—an excellent book offering insight into how to effectively run an Internet business and maximize profits.

Lease-Versus-Buy Software

- PlanEase software analyzes every type of real estate transaction. Free demo at www.planease.com/default.aspx
- "Lease Mod" has MS Excel templates for analysis in real estate decisions. Free demo at www.lsemod.com/index.html

Tax Laws and Information for Small Businesses

- Robert G. Allen, one of the wealthiest men in America, has his lawyer's top ten tips for small businesses available at www.robertgallen.com/taxcut.php.
- The IRS's one-stop resource for small businesses: www.irs.gov/businesses/small/index.html
- Great article from Kiplinger online about saving money on taxes for home-based businesses: www.kiplinger.com/features/archives/2007/01/workathome.html

Zoning

- Your local courthouse is the best resource for local laws, zoning, and information about your area.

[Strategy 6]

The High-Performance Entrepreneur Is Web Savvy

Barbara Lyngarkos, MBA

The Internet is the Viagra of big business.
Jack Welch

Everyone is talking about the Internet. It's fun! It's exciting! Moreover, it's not just for kids. The Internet, particularly in its graphic interface known as the World Wide Web, is probably the most important communication vehicle developed since the telephone. Most importantly for the small business, the Web levels the playing field between small businesses and conglomerates.

The Web is the newest medium for advertising. It offers significant advantages over traditional advertising media in that it is dynamic, interactive, and inexpensive. The Internet is making it possible for small- to medium-sized businesses to compete with the corporate establishments. Of course, as the Web matures, advertising rates for the most popular sites will increase. Advertising is not the only way to make your business known via the Web. Search engines are another powerful and low-cost way to increase awareness of your products and services.

E-Commerce: The Newest Business Frontier (It's Time to Get Connected)

If you have not decided whether the fanfare over conducting business online is hype or reality and are holding off developing a Web site for your enterprise, you could be missing a powerful business tool.

The Internet is proving to be a significant business leveler, allowing small and medium-size companies to compete with the giants on the same global playing field. Whether your business provides services or goods, some of the most efficient marketing and selling tools are available via the Internet, and the potential of reaching a vast audience is open to you through the World Wide Web. Consider

81

these facts: Ipsos, a market research company, estimates that in 2004, there were 162 million Americans using the Internet. Now that's a market!

Time-starved consumers are becoming more comfortable using credit and bankcards to make purchases from security-backed virtual retailers. They comparison shop over the Internet for the best quality and cost and purchase a range of goods from groceries to high-tech products.

As the electronic-consumer trade continues to soar, business-to-business e-commerce will be even stronger. Many larger corporations have already mandated the use of online transactions to their downstream vendors. According to the SBA, the introduction of electronic commerce in federal contracting is moving ahead, and small business owners must adopt this new business strategy to remain fully competitive.

Until recently, developing an e-commerce Web site meant dealing with multiple companies: one to develop the Web site, one for e-commerce integration, one to host the site, and yet another provider for secure payment processing. Now, you can develop your own Web site in a matter of hours.

Check out www.HiPerWebSolutions.com for some of the lowest prices on do-it-yourself Web site packages, domain names, e-marketing products, and many other Web site based products. Additionally, all customers receive 24/7 customer support along with many free add-ons.

General Offers and Claims Products and Services

The Federal Trade Commission Act allows the FTC to act in the interest of all consumers to prevent deceptive and unfair acts or practices. In interpreting Section 5 of the act, the commission has determined that a representation, omission, or practice is deceptive if it is likely to:

- Mislead consumers, or
- Affect consumers' behavior or decisions about the product or service

In addition, an act or practice is unfair if the injury it causes, or is likely to cause, is:

- Substantial
- Not outweighed by other benefits
- Not reasonably avoidable

The FTC Act prohibits unfair or deceptive advertising in any medium. That is, advertising must tell the truth and not mislead consumers. A claim can be misleading if relevant information is left out or if the claim implies something that is not true. For example, a lease advertisement for an automobile that promotes "$0 down" may be misleading if significant and undisclosed charges are due at lease signing.

In addition, claims must be substantiated, especially when they concern health, safety, or performance. The type of evidence may depend on the product, the claims, and what experts believe necessary. If your ad specifies a certain level of support for a claim—"tests show X"—you must have at least that level of support.

Sellers are responsible for claims they make about their products and services. Third parties—such as advertising agencies, Web site designers, and catalog marketers—also may be liable for making or disseminating deceptive representations if they participate in the preparation or distribution of the advertising, or know about the deceptive claims.

- Advertising agencies and Web site designers are responsible for reviewing the information used to substantiate ad claims. They may not simply rely on an advertiser's assurance that the claims are substantiated. In determining whether an ad agency should be held liable, the FTC looks at the extent of the agency's participation in the preparation of the challenged ad and whether the agency knew or should have known that the ad included false or deceptive claims.

- To protect themselves, catalog marketers should ask for material to back up claims rather than repeat what the manufacturer says about the product. If the manufacturer does not come forward with proof or turns over proof that looks questionable, the catalog marketer should see a yellow caution light and proceed appropriately, especially when it comes to extravagant performance claims, health or weight loss promises, or earnings guarantees. In writing ad copy, catalogers should stick to claims that can be supported. Most important, catalog marketers should trust their instincts when a product sounds too good to be true.

Other Points to Consider

Disclaimers and disclosures must be clear and conspicuous. That is, consumers must be able to notice, read or hear, and understand the information. Still, a disclaimer or disclosure alone usually is not enough to remedy a false or deceptive claim.

- Demonstrations must show how the product will perform under normal use.

- Refunds must be made to dissatisfied consumers if you promised to make them.

- Advertising directed to children raises special issues. That is because children may have greater difficulty evaluating advertising claims and understanding the nature of the information you provide. Sellers should take special care not to misrepresent a product or its performance when advertising to children. The Children's Advertising Review Unit (CARU) of the Council of Better Business Bureaus has published specific guidelines for children's advertising that you may find helpful.

Information About Online Advertising, an FTC staff paper, provides additional information for online advertisers. The paper discusses the factors used to evaluate the clarity and conspicuousness of required disclosures in online ads. It also discusses how certain FTC rules and guides that uses terms like "writing" or "printed" apply to Internet activities and how technologies such as e-mail may be used to comply with certain rules and guides.

Protecting Consumers' Privacy Online

The Internet provides unprecedented opportunities for the collection and sharing of information from and about consumers, but studies show that consumers have very strong concerns about the security and confidentiality of their personal information in the online marketplace. Many consumers also report being wary of engaging in online commerce, in part because they fear that their personal information can be misused.

These consumer concerns present an opportunity for you to build on consumer trust by implementing effective, voluntary, industry-wide practices to protect consumers' information privacy. The FTC has held a number of workshops for industry, consumer groups, and privacy advocates to explore industry guidelines to protect consumers' privacy online.

E-commerce, e-tailing, Internet business ... they are all names for business that is conducted through the Internet. There are literally millions of online businesses, but for every successful venture, there are many, many failures. Whether the business will be completely online, or an extension of a brick-and-mortar presence, there are several steps that should be taken to facilitate a positive, profitable experience.

Choosing a Web Host

Investigating Web host providers can be a daunting task. There are so many available that it is difficult to compare them side by side. Prior to starting your research, a checklist should be made so each provider is compared using the same scale. That checklist should include:

Reliability: A good host will guarantee uptime to be at least 99 percent of the time. Without this guarantee, the host has no incentive to maintain their servers.

Format: Web hosting is available in three different formats. Virtual terminals host several sites on one computer. Dedicated servers are used for high-traffic businesses, and managed, dedicated servers are also available. Virtual terminals are inexpensive, but may lack sufficient resources to efficiently host business sites. Dedicated servers are the most expensive and require in-house management. Managed, dedicated servers are a mid-line choice where sites are hosted on many computers. When one server fails, another server takes over with no downtime.

Bandwidth: Once the server type is decided, data transfer or "bandwidth" should be considered. This determines how much data can be transferred to and from the site. Some companies offer limited bandwidth for a reduced price, but the fine print reveals that if the site exceeds the limits, extravagant charges may be levied (similar to roaming charges on a cell phone). For a typical small business just starting out, 3GB of bandwidth should be sufficient. Be sure to know what is involved in adding bandwidth and additional related costs if necessary. Even hosts who offer unlimited data transfer sometimes whack you with extraneous charges. Be sure to read the fine print.

Dedicated space: The amount of space dedicated to a business determines how many products and files you can accommodate. Typically, 5–15 MB of dedicated space is needed for a small- to medium-sized business. Once again, you must read the fine print and be sure you are aware of any and all charges that might apply if you go over or need to make changes.

Software compatibility: You must be sure that the host can accommodate any specific files that may already be in place or construction. Microsoft Expression Web extensions are important if you are using it to develop your site. Other software may have specific requirements that need to be met as well.

Connection: Connection types vary by provider and should be determined to evaluate the speed at which your site will operate. A slow connection will frustrate your customers and will result in reduced sales. There are several types of connections—of those, a T3 is the fastest. A T1 is also very fast and acceptable. A dial-up connection is not functional for a business.

Customer service/technical help: The level of customer service the host provides is extremely important. Many offer 24/7 availability. Be sure the provider offers sufficient customer service options to meet the company's needs. Problems always seem to arise at the most inopportune times. Be sure you are covered. It does not hurt to call the customer service and technical service lines to make sure you are happy with the response quality provided.

E-mail and auto-responders: The number of e-mail addresses you are allowed affects the transfer of information. You need to have enough addresses so mail can be disseminated to the appropriate area. Many one-person operations use different e-mail addresses to pre-sort their mail. One for customer service, one for sales, one for technical assistance, etc. The ability to forward e-mail is also important. Some providers offer up to a thousand e-mail addresses, such as seen at www. HiPerWebSolutions.com.

Auto-responders are helpful to let your customer know that their e-mail has been received and will be addressed. Many other uses for auto-responders make them an important part of the e-commerce solution. An auto-responder may also be used to send out mini instructional programs customers register for on your Web site. The auto-responder can be programmed to send out a new lesson every day or however often you program it for.

Design services: Web site design software is offered by many hosts and can be as easy as filling in the blanks or as hard as writing your own script. You can choose the best plan that matches your expertise. Many also offer complete design services. Many hosts also provide packages that include a build-it-yourself Web site. These may also come with e-mail addresses, hosting, domain names, and several other e-commerce related services.

Multi-media, CGI scripts, and forms are offered by most providers, but often at an increased cost. You can determine whether these services will be advantageous and decide accordingly.

Data backups: Data backups are a necessary part of the online experience. This is a service that is extremely important. Data must be backed up regularly to offset impending disaster. If your provider does not offer this service, it must be addressed in-house. Let one server malfunction occur, and if your site has not been backed up, there goes all your hard work.

Server: The type of server the host is using should be investigated to be sure it is compatible with the type of site you wish to build. There are Windows based servers as well as Apache servers, and each offers a host of features.

Opinions and reviews: Search out opinions and reviews on Web host providers. Actual experience with a host can be enlightening and will expose shortcomings. Be sure to use review sites that are impartial and are not getting paid by the hosts. One such company is www.Whreviews.com. You will find a plethora of information relating to hosting services and choosing the best one for your situation. It can also be helpful to open and participate in blogs or forums about each host. You will also find Web tutorials on this helpful site.

Statistics/log files: Many hosts offer statistics relating to site use that can be very useful. Logs and statistics can help to determine which parts of the site are successful and which parts need attention. These statistics can also be used in conjunction with marketing efforts.

Expandability: Make sure the ability to expand and upgrade is available at minimal additional cost.

Costs and contract terms: A comparison of costs should be made; be sure that the prices you are comparing include the same levels of services. Contract terms should be investigated and scrutinized for any verbiage that may inhibit your level of control over your site. Find out upfront if there are charges for moving to another host. These charges can be steep and are not usually readily advertised. Working with a popular, well-known host should alleviate most worries about hidden costs, but it is still prudent to be diligent about reading the fine print.

Securing a Domain Name

ICAAN (Internet Corporation for Assigned Names and Numbers) is responsible for the worldwide coordination of domain names. A domain name is a unique identifier that allows other computers to identify and access your site. A dedicated domain should be as short as possible and may contain both letters and symbols. The name should be easy to remember and easy to spell. With the explosion of

Internet businesses created every day, the name must grab the attention of the customer and compel them to visit the site. The name you choose will serve to identify and brand your company.

Customer demographics should also be considered when creating the name to make it attractive to the target audience. Domain names may be purchased in different increments of time (i.e., one year, two years, five years, ten years). It is up to the company who registers the name to renew at the appropriate time. Failure to do so could result in the permanent loss of the domain name.

Whether or not the company has an existing name, several variations for the domain name should be considered as some names may already be taken. If the company already has a name, the same name would likely be the first choice for the online presence as well. If the name desired is not available, an offer to purchase the name could be made, or a close but not exactly similar name can be formulated. A startup business must choose a name based on the purpose of the company. Customers will identify the company by its name.

There are many extensions available today. Many businesses will register several with their name to keep the name as exclusive as possible. Internet business names in the United States typically end in *.com*. Other countries have their own particular format that can be investigated through ICAAN. Some typical extensions are used to identify the particular type of entity that it represents. For instance, *.org* is typically used for non-profit organizations, and *.edu* is used by educational institutions. New extensions are being developed, and information relating to this subject can be found on the ICAAN site.

When registering your company name, use caution. Stay away from using sub-domain names. A sub-domain name might look like Mybusines@anotherbusiness.com. Not only are sub-domain names owned by the companies that issue them, the names are long and cumbersome for customers to use. The use of a sub-domain name inhibits the ability to move your site and keep the same name. While they are inexpensive, most successful businesses will outgrow these services and will have to start a new site with a new name. This will disrupt business and could cause severe financial strain. The price for domain names can be as low as $4.00 for a *.biz* domain, or $40.00 for a domain from China.

There are numerous dedicated domain name registrars that can be found with an online search. Check the ICAAN site (www.icaan.org) to be sure the domain name registrar you have chosen is approved. Do not use a registrar who is not approved by ICAAN. This can lead to temporary or possibly permanent loss of your domain name. The provider mentioned earlier, www.HiPerWebSolutions. com, is approved by ICANN and offers some of the lowest prices.

Choosing a Shopping Cart

Shopping cart software is often offered in conjunction with hosting services. Shopping carts can be hosted or licensed. A hosted cart is essentially a rented cart where a monthly fee is paid for use. Outright purchase of the shopping cart software is referred to as licensed. Outright purchase allows the cart to be moved; hosted carts have to be re-worked in the new format when changing providers, though it is a far less expensive upfront cost. When deciding on an independent shopping cart, consider the ease of interface with your site. You may find a cheaper solution than the one your current host offers, but if it doesn't integrate easily, it will cost much more in the long run. The number of items your company will sell is one of the most important considerations when researching shopping cart services. Some limit the number of products you may list and charge substantial fees if you increase your product offerings. Be sure to allow for growth and expansion.

Look at live stores powered by several shopping carts. This can be a good place to determine the preferred look and feel of the cart. Determine what management tools are offered and be sure to find out all of the costs involved. Many shopping carts offer services à la carte. You need to get an idea of the total cost to be able to compare apples to apples.

Payment and shipping components of the shopping cart should be investigated to be sure that the proper configurations are available. If you plan to ship internationally, you must be sure the shopping cart can accommodate this. UPS, Federal Express, and the USPS rates are integrated into many shopping carts. To do this manually can be time consuming and aggravating.

Some providers offer free trials so you can make sure the product will work with your particular needs. This is a great way to investigate the nuances of several carts prior to making a decision. Lastly, be sure that the shopping cart integrates with the chosen accounting software. This will aid in seamless financial control and reduce redundancy.

Merchant Services

Merchant services and real-time credit card processing are essential as credit cards are the most popular form of payment on the Internet. Over the last several years, credit card security has been heightened, enabling consumers a feeling of safety concerning use over the Internet. Placing your security policy where it can be easily viewed will also boost the confidence of potential buyers. Most times, security icons are posted at the bottom of your main page.

Merchant services can be contracted in conjunction with a payment gateway service, or they can be contracted separately. Typically, it is in the best interest of the business to try to contract the two services from the same provider so compatibility is ensured. In the long run, costs are more likely to be less as well. The merchant service enables the processing of the credit cards, and the payment gateway enables the actual financial transaction to occur.

Typical charges are a monthly fee, a per-transaction fee, and a percentage of the sale, commonly called the discount rate. Merchant service providers who promise diamond service at a rhinestone price are usually not a good choice. They typically have rolling reserve policies, higher chargeback fees, and other hidden costs. It is a good idea to research many providers and take note of more than just the price. Any additional fees that may be charged for unusual transactions should be compared, and customer service and technical help availability are extremely important.

Merchant services can include online as well as offline processing. Online processing is in real time and reduces the redundancy of offline processing where customers fill in forms that are processed at a later time. It also allows instant verification of the card, reducing the chance of fraudulent transactions. Offline transactions should always be authorized prior to shipping or sending the actual product.

If the business has a current merchant service provider, check with them to see if they also offer online services. Often, packages are available that are less expensive than contracting two separate merchant services accounts. Consider more than just the cost when choosing a merchant services provider.

The availability of easily administered processes and the hardware needed to perform those services should be determined to consider the entire system cost before making a decision. Again, be sure that all components are compatible, including currently used accounting software. Be especially cautious if you are planning on using a laptop computer. Some point of sale hardware will not work on laptops.

Site Design

Site maps, storyboards, and schematics can be used to document the proposed structure of the site. It is a good idea to use handwritten visuals when first designing the site. It is easy to visualize the site map as a whole when the entire idea is in front of you. Software should be used after the basic prototype has been designed.

Unique content is the key to a popular Web site. Start collecting on-topic, relevant information as soon as possible. If you are not a proficient writer, hire a copywriter. The presentation of the information needs to be interesting as well. It is not recommended that site design be done in-house unless someone has actual design experience. Many hosts offer design services starting from a minimal amount of help to as much as complete design services. Template-driven sites are available, but may limit creativity.

Site design must be managed to produce a consumer-oriented and friendly experience. There is no substitute for excellent customer service. Web site design principles must address a service-oriented ambiance while promoting customer attraction and retention. Particular attention must be paid to detail inclusion and smooth maneuverability within the site. The physical look of the site must be attractive to catch the customers' attention. The information contained in the site and the ease of site navigation will determine the retention rate of the site. The content you provide must answer a need of the customer. You should strive to provide comprehensive yet concise content.

Organization is critical to the user-friendly interface required for online success. Information should be organized in a logical manner using interesting verbiage. A search feature should be incorporated as well as navigational buttons. You should use color and texture consistently throughout your site to provide a compatible look and feel. Uniqueness of design, logos, and layouts that will distinguish the site from others, should be consistent and must load quickly. Be sure to test your site on different Web connections to troubleshoot every aspect of the customer experience.

Usability of the site is second only to the ability of the verbiage to elicit an image in the potential consumer's mind that excites and entices the consumer to keep reading. Consult sites of similar businesses, competitors, and other well-known popular sites. Notice how the products are presented, what works and what doesn't. Remember that you are also a consumer and your opinion counts. Talk to friends and existing or potential customers to get a feel for what is important and what is not.

Design services are available to relieve you from the effort to complete the site design. Many hosting services offer template-driven software that is easy to use and affordable. The design needs to be versatile and adaptable to the changes that will take place during the life of the business. The best solution is to research the many options available and use the one that is within the budget and fits the needs of the business plan.

Organization, display, and a level of atmosphere built into the site will draw the customer's attention. There is no difference between merchandising on the

Internet or in a store window. Both must create interest and enthusiasm about the product. The use of color, available information, and graphics must coordinate to make the customer feel compelled to seek more information about the product. Site design must anticipate customer needs and provide the information to foster action.

A special area for customers to post testimonials or success stories is a way for customers to share their stories. This could be interlaced with a blog or forum area.

After the site is designed and tweaked to perfection, it must be launched and registered with the various search engines to establish a presence on the World Wide Web. Search engines are likened to spiders crawling around their web. They move through sites and look for certain keywords that are used to index the sites. Those indexes are what determine the placement of information in search results.

Use of Key Words

Keyword use is an art and takes a lot of research to determine the best words to optimize. There are many sites that offer advice and claim to know the secrets to keyword success. The fact is that search engines are constantly changing the way sites are indexed, so there are no shortcuts to optimize a site. Tools are available to assist with keyword and search engine optimization (SEO) and should be used on a regular basis.

Wordtracker.com offers a free trial for keyword generating software. Once keywords are determined, it is a good idea to use them as links instead of graphics, and to name the pages with keywords rather than generic names. Keywords should also be used in the site content, but be careful not to overuse them. There are differing opinions on just how many keywords are optimal. Some sites that offer free SEO tools include trafficjams.com and keyworddensity.com. Tools offered by Google Webmaster Central are free and relatively easy to use. Your host may also offer services to help in this area. Vertical search engines are cropping up within many industries and can be another source of new customers.

Keep in mind that the design of the site must be flexible to easily allow updates and changes. Links should be checked for accuracy and the site should be refreshed at least once a month. New, relevant, and fresh content will bring customers back time after time. An archive can be set up to house older, well-visited information. Lastly, the files use on your site may be saved as PDF or Microsoft Word document.

Privacy and Security

Privacy and security issues are important to the successful operation of an Internet business. A privacy statement should tell the customer exactly what you intend to do with the information collected during the sales process. It should be specific and attempt to reduce the fear of the consumer with regard to their private information.

The security of the checkout transaction is of the utmost importance, and an SSL, or security certificate, is required to provide secure transactions for your customers. Some shopping cart providers offer security certificates as part of their packages. If yours does not, you must secure a certificate from a Certificate Authority (CA). In the United States, CAs include VeriSign, Entrust, and Equifax. In Europe, you must visit www.EEMA.org to secure your certificate. Check out www.HiPerWebSolutions.com for information and great deals on CAs of SSLs.

A security statement should address the measures taken to ensure transaction security. Customers should leave the site feeling that their personal information is safe and secure. Creating and displaying these policies will secure a trusting customer base who will feel confident when placing online orders. Most sites place a security logo at the bottom of the main page. Doing this allows customers to know that you are providing top security for their personal information.

Marketing

Sales are all about creating and sustaining a relationship with your customers. Knowing where to spend your marketing dollars to gain the maximum return on investment is important to facilitate relationship building. Evaluate all opportunities before making any decisions on a plan. Marketing a Web site is based on the same premise as marketing an offline business. Grab the customers' attention to peak their interest in the products being sold. Standard marketing practices can be applied as well as many online techniques that have become popular. The key is to prepare an informed marketing plan to be used as a compass to maintain focus as new marketing opportunities arise.

A situational or S.W.O.T. (Strengths, Weaknesses, Opportunities, and Threats) analysis must be investigated and should include information on current opportunities and characteristics of the e-market, factors affecting success, a competitors' analysis, legal, social, and technological factors as well as possible problems that may arise. Do not forget to address the strengths and weaknesses of the current company. Tactical marketing choices are numerous and need to be evaluated for application and consistency. Keeping this information in mind will ensure that strategic focus will evolve as the site is developed. Strategies regarding pricing, distribution, price, and promotion are an important part of the process.

Once the needed information is gathered, several marketing techniques can be used to optimize the site's effectiveness. Building a mailing list using information collected is a way to begin a customer-based marketing program. This can be done through a sign up area on your home page where visitors can opt-in. Online newsletters or e-zines and e-mail advertising can be offered using a double opt-in, opt-out procedure. This means that the customer must acknowledge to you two times that they are interested in receiving your communications. The communications must also include an opt-out choice so customers can discontinue participation.

A forward to a friend feature could be added to encourage the customer to share the information with their friends. Surveys can be sent to existing and potential customers to gather information, and incentives can be offered to increase participation. List management software is often included with shopping cart software or may be purchased separately. Personalization lends a friendly and effective catch to communications. It makes the consumer feel important and increases the likelihood that they will consider returning to the site for a possible purchase. Keep in mind that communications must be targeted and not sent randomly.

Unsolicited communications are in conflict with anti-spam regulations that are now being enforced. Ignoring this issue could lead to blacklisting your site. It is a good idea to become familiar with anti-spam regulations. A good way to test the effectiveness of an e-mail campaign is to randomly select a small percentage of your mailing list. Send one version of the campaign to half of the addresses and another version to the balance. This is an easy way to see which will be more affective prior to sending the communication to the entire list.

Pay-per-click advertising allows a company to bid on a keyword that then places the company's information at the top of Web search results. Google, eBay, and MSN all have pay-per-click programs.

Other marketing trends include linking with other sites, even with competitors. These links can help generate traffic and allow your site to be listed higher with search engines. It is important to link only with relevant sites so the customer base will be interested in the products being sold. Banner ads should be catchy and graphic with the words "click here" visible. Simple animation and humor can increase click through rates that typically average 1.5 to 2.5 percent.

Affiliate sales can be beneficial, but you must be careful about the quality of the affiliate sites. Choose appropriate affiliate programs by evaluating payouts, honesty, and general theme of the affiliate. Question whether it fits in with the general theme you are trying to generate. Cross-selling and up-selling are pertinent methods of suggestive selling that, when used affectively, can generate additional sales. When having a special sale, create a Web-landing page designed just for that purpose.

Conclusion

When starting a Web business, research several alternatives before choosing providers. Be sure to read the fine print so there are no surprises down the road. Talk to other people who have a Web presence and get opinions on best practices. Read, read, read; there is so much information available and much of it is free and aids in good decision making. Be sure to check the compatibility of all the hardware and software before you purchase. Fixing incompatibility issues after purchase is next to impossible.

Resources

Web Hosting and Domain Registration

- www.hiperwebsolutions.com

General

- www.practicalecommerce.com
- www.microsoft.com/smallbusiness
- www.about.com
- www.entrepreneur.com
- www.ecommercetimes.com

Site Development

- www.google.com/webmasters
- www.trafficjams.com
- www.keyworddensity.com
- www.hiperwebsolutions.com

Security

- www.verisign.com
- www.entrust.com
- www.equifax.com
- www.hiperwebsolutions.com

Books

- *The Art of Digital Branding.* Corcoran, I. (2007). New York: Allworth Press.
- *Guerilla Marketing Research.* Kaden, R. J. (2006). Philadelphia: Kogan Page USA.
- *Sign Me Up! A Marketer's Guide to Email Newsletters That Build Relationships and Boost Sales.* Matt Blumberg, T. M. (2006). New York: iUniverse.
- *The Complete E-Commerce Book.* Reynolds, J. (2004). San Francisco: CMP Books.
- *The Unofficial Guide to Starting a Business Online.* Rich, J. R. (2000). Hoboken, New Jersey: Wiley.

[Strategy 7]

The High-Performance Entrepreneur Executes Leadership

Michael B. Meek, MSM

You're never beaten until you admit it.
General George S. Patton

Leadership is an overused word that has come to mean so many things both positive and negative. Ask twenty people what they think of when they think of a leader and you're likely to get twenty different responses. What does leadership mean to *you*? Who is more of a leader—someone who is so smart he seems to always have all of the answers, or someone who has made so many mistakes he can speak from experience? If you believe all of the books you read on leadership, which are many, you'll find that either one can be an effective leader.

Did you see the "Book Smarts vs. Street Smarts" episode of Donald Trump's TV show, *The Apprentice*? The two camps were equally matched. It seems to me that books about leadership seem to tell us much of the same thing over and again. There is no shortage of information on the subject; just look it up on the Internet and you'll find enough material to read for the next three years.

My contention with the leadership gurus of today isn't so much whether they are right or wrong about what a leader is; my contention is that I'm not sure there's one right answer. It seems to me that for every theory or personality profile assessment, you can find one that is exactly contrary to that opinion. One person can write a book and spend his whole life speaking to audiences about his theory, while the next woman comes along and spends her career teaching principles that fly in the face of his logic. They both seem to know what they're talking about, so who is right?

Does someone have to be wrong? I'm not sure they do. Leadership isn't so much about style, principles, or theory; it's about execution. It's about being able to apply what you know and having the ability to rally those around you toward a common cause. That ability to rally people can look very different for each leader.

Just look at the world today. How can different individuals with such different styles all yield results? Because it isn't about the style, it's about the execution.

I contend that a leader must execute or die. My meaning can be found in the phrase, *Execute Means Application.* If I apply my leadership abilities, I will be effective and gain results. If I don't apply them, I will die in my leadership role. I will be ineffective and therefore lose the support of those I lead; I will die as a leader. I don't even think it matters what type of person you are—your morals, principals, beliefs, or habits. You can find an effective leader who will fall into any category you research. Why? Because they know how to execute! I also believe that some people are effective leaders and never realize it. Some individuals have small leadership roles. They are so good, so respected in a specific area that others want to follow them, but they don't know how to execute, therefore are never viewed as a leader.

You Have to Love It Forever

What does it take to execute? One must have *passion* about something. You can't rally the troops around a common cause without passion. This doesn't mean you have to be charismatic, this means you must be passionate about your cause. Passion isn't something you can conjure up at a moment's time; you either are or you aren't passionate about something. I believe this is a prerequisite to being a leader; not many people will follow someone who doesn't have the ability to show this passion. Passion comes from the ability to care about something that is greater than you are, whatever it may be.

You must have *persistence.* No leader is able to have everything go his way all of the time, so persistence is crucial. It's walking in the valley of failure in life that makes us stronger, it's not the successes. How much do we really learn from the things that come easy—what is there to learn from? The leader who gets knocked down and gets up again and again, each time with more determination, will succeed.

You must understand the importance of *follow-through.* This does not mean that a leader has to be good at following through themselves; it means the leader must be good at ensuring that follow-through happens. A senior vice-president for a national financial institute is a client and a dear friend. This individual's ability to follow through is as poor as any one of the thirty thousand people I've worked with over the last two decades. However, he is a great leader; he knows his weaknesses and fills those gaps by surrounding himself with a team that completes him.

You must show yourself to be *strong*. This can be done in many ways, whether your strength is physical, social, psychological, emotional, or your work ethic. I've seen leaders with a quiet strength about them who were twice as effective as the vocal motivational leader. If you break down each of these strengths, you find out a lot about how leaders execute:

- *Physical Strength.* This can be done by mere presence; you can use your size to cast fear into others supporting you. You can use your looks to charm them into following you. You can do as Lance Armstrong is known for, out-pain them into following. In his book, Lance describes why he has been so successful since his rehabilitation from cancer. He explains how no one else is willing to endure as much pain as he is; therefore, he wins by breaking down his opponent. He gains much respect by this tactic, but also many enemies. Why is that so? How can a leader be so liked and accepted by one group, only to be hated by another?

- *Social Strength.* A leader can use his or her speech to gain followers. Former President Clinton comes to mind; I've never seen anyone who could so effectively use his social speaking ability to gain support after he violated moral code after moral code. Another leader may use her social status or connections to gain support, while someone else may be an effective leader because of his generosity. My wife is one who fits this category; I've never met a human being more willing to give of themselves to others in need at any time for any reason. For this, she gains a level of respect that classifies her as a leader.

- *Psychological Strength.* One can use their mental skills and knowledge to gain followers. How many of us have met those people who seem to know something about everything? It doesn't matter what the subject, they can speak logically about it. I've seen one person who is loathed because he doesn't know how to do this effectively, while another is respected and people love to have him be a part of any conversation they are in. Other leaders use their ability to read people to gain followers; they seem to always know what you're thinking before you ever speak a word. Then of course, there are the people who think they know what you're thinking and finish your sentences for you. Which one do you think is effective?

- *Emotional Strength.* Many leaders possess an emotional strength that can be seen in both the charismatic and the soft-spoken. One leader can emotionally lose control and fear people into submission, although it's only effective in the short term. This usually doesn't work well in non third-world countries. How many times do we see the clergy show an emotional outpour to their congregation in repentance and the followers get in line? In crisis situations, the leader who shows no emotions at all, but calmly focuses on the task at hand until the solution is implemented, gains followers at that moment and in the future.

- *Work Ethic.* Some leaders just lead by example; their work ethic is so good that others want to emulate them. They are respected for this work ethic by the majority, while the minority that isn't willing to strive for that level of effort is critical of them. Yet, others take it too far (workaholics); no one wants to follow them, as they seem to never understand there are limits and that balance is important.

Smoke and Mirrors

A leader who is willing to admit his vulnerabilities shows great strength. This is so contrary to the visual of the General Patton image many grew up with. I'm not saying you need to have a therapy session with those you lead, but that you let them know that you know you're human. We've all heard the phrase, *perception is reality.* This is so true; your perception is your reality, regardless of the truth or the facts. How many perceptions are based upon non-truths? Every day, we make judgments of others based on how they look, what they drive, what they're wearing, how they carry themselves, and what someone else told us (which is rarely true).

We are such a shallow society in so many ways. Hollywood tells us how we should look or what is cool by their standards. This impacts our lives, and leaders have to acknowledge that people base decisions on things this shallow. So what's the point? It is that as a leader, it's important that your self-esteem is large enough that you don't worry about what others think of you, but that you are in tune enough with their perceptions that you can manage them. Managing their perceptions is important to ensure they have the real facts about you, or it can hurt your cause. Leaders spend more time on this one issue than anything else. Even conflict resolution necessitates managing people's perceptions.

Leadership execution is "leading by example." But what does that mean? I can tell this best through the stories of others I've witnessed over the years. One gentleman, who has a personal net worth of millions of dollars and owns numerous companies, took me to one of his plants. As he entered, he introduced me to the receptionist and began giving me a tour. He shook hands with every employee he walked by that day; it took us about two hours just to go through the facility. He knew most of their names, he looked them straight in the eye when he spoke to them, and he gave them his full attention for the thirty seconds he stood in front of them.

It was an amazing experience to see a leader who has thousands of employees and more responsibility than I'd ever understand spend that time with those employees. I've seen bank presidents spend half a day a month working the front teller line and making it a requirement for all management. This to me is the epitome of leading by example—rolling your sleeves up and being willing to get your hands dirty doing the real work that makes your organization successful. Let's face it, how much time does a leader spend doing the "dirty" work? Most of a leader's time is spent planning, communicating, coordinating, problem solving, networking, relationship building, and delegating.

Ask yourself when the last time was you did the work of those you lead? The answer may scare you—it may have been so long, and you may not even be *able* to do the work (if you wanted to) with the changes in technology, systems, and processes. This leads us to another key area for a leader: change management.

A Little Change Will Do You Good

Change is inevitable; any leader who can't adapt to it, or in many cases cause it, will fail. This is a truth that is becoming more and more evident. Our parents grew up in a world of much more certainty. The world looked different; they didn't fear going to school, their spiritual leader was the real thing, the temptations weren't near as prevalent, and they didn't fear being shot by a coworker. Their coworker had been working with them for years since they'd both been at the same company most of their lives.

Today's environment of limited loyalty on both sides, the employee and the employer, has created a reason for change. With the constant rotation of the workforce, employers need to systematize and standardize the work so that they can train a new employee relatively quickly to perform the task. This, coupled with the technology changes that occur seemingly weekly, makes managing change extremely difficult for many leaders. Personalities do impact one's ability to handle change, and a leader is no different—some are much better than others at this.

One core trait for a leader to effectively handle change is *the ability to confront.* The leader's ability to confront issues head-on is crucial to his success in handling change. Many leaders are afraid of confrontation. The idea of holding another adult accountable for his actions is less than attractive to them. Accountability can come in so many forms, but it holds a negative connotation, since we usually don't have to worry about accountability if everyone is doing what they're supposed to when they're suppose to do it. This is one of the areas for improvement for many leaders.

Leadership Execution: The DCA Way

Now that we've looked at some of the issues and some of the requirements for execution, how is it done? If you try to simplify all of the things required for effective leadership into three categories, they would be what we call the **DCA Model**: *Direction, Communication,* and *Accountability.*

Direction

Direction is the leader's first order of business. If the people being led don't know the direction of the company, how do they know where to follow? How do they know where to go? Which way is success? Can I even get there from here? We begin by working directly with the highest level of leadership. In some organizations, this is the board of directors; in others, it is the executive or management team. Whichever applies, it is crucial that it be the highest level. We find most management teams that report to a board don't have a clearly defined direction they operate from, which obviously creates many problems.

The first exercise my team does when working with leaders is to ask each core leader to write down what they believe the "goal" of the organization is. We have yet to work with a single company where each leader identified the same goal; this is out of three hundred and fifty organizations, mind you. If the top leaders of an organization aren't on the same page, how can they expect the rest of the organization to follow in step? The direction of the company has to be so clearly defined that it is a rallying point.

I remember very clearly the first day of practice on my college football team. The first thing we did was hold a team meeting where the head coach stood in the front of the room and asked what the goal for that year was. After much brainstorming, debate, and lots of blank stares, the team settled on making the playoffs. That became the rallying point. We worked very hard that year and constantly focused on that "mission" of the team. We made the playoffs and lost in the first round. The next year, we had the same meeting and the goal became to win the national championship. That university I attended has become one of the most successful football programs in all of college football over the last two decades. I believe this is largely because of the leadership's ability to provide a clear direction for the team to rally behind.

Communication

Communication is the next order of business. Once the direction is in rallying point form, communicating it effectively must occur throughout the entire organization. This is where you get buy-in. Once the employees know where it is you want to go and you've effectively communicated it, now they can be involved with figuring out how you're going to get there.

My college football team didn't talk about the national championship every day; we talked about the next game and had game plans of how we were going to accomplish one game at a time all the way to the championship ring. The planning phase is where employees can be involved in the development of the strategic plan, which is crucial since they are the ones who are going to be implementing most of it. Once the plan is in place and the direction set, hold weekly huddles for the whole company, led by each front line leader. This is the opportunity for the leadership team to keep each employee informed as to what is going on in relation to the direction that was set forth.

Accountability

Accountability is what ties it all together. I've seen several organizations that do a good job with direction and communication, but rarely see any that do well with accountability. This is where the rubber meets the road; this is where the idea and vision people struggle because it's where the doing actually gets done. Every action should have specified deadlines with responsible parties, and in our DCA model, you communicate in the weekly huddles the status of the plan.

So, this is where we become accountable to each other and to the process; no matter what happens, I have to communicate to everyone in the company where I'm at in the area I'm responsible for. The DCA can be a form of accountability in just daily communication. You should end every conversation you have with each other with a DCA, "Is there any more *direction* you need from me? Any more *communication* that needs to occur either way? What is the *accountability;* who is doing what and by when?" A leader can't go very long without executing and not being caught in this model. It weeds through those who are capable of executing and those who aren't in short order.

I believe in action teams where employees are part of the problem solving as well. A task may be given to a team of three to five to work on; everyone in the company knows who is on the action team, what the team's objective is, and that the team members are the representatives for the company. If anyone has any ideas or feedback for the issue being worked on, they must present it to one of the action team members, and that team member is to then represent those ideas. In essence, this simple model allows you to involve the entire organization in solving certain problems, leading to buy-in throughout. An agenda item in the weekly huddle is to discuss the status of each action team, keeping everyone informed.

Those who fear bureaucracy, I hear you loud and clear. This process can be very rewarding, but it has to be managed so that teams are effective and don't become bogged down in nonessential agenda items. Teams that aren't effective are to be disbanded. My history shows that about 85 percent of action team recommendations are adopted by management. When employees are part of the planning process, it makes accountability so much easier for the leader.

One such example is a company that was having attendance problems. An action team was put together that consisted of three of the best employees and one of the worst attendance abusers. That team put a policy in place that was much harsher than management would have ever dreamed of implementing. They even had to tone it down a bit. The result was that the poor-attendance employee dramatically improved and the entire attitude about attendance changed in the company. How were employees going to argue a policy that was put together by the employees? And employees couldn't argue they had no say in it because it was discussed at the weekly huddles and the action team members were their representatives.

Make Your Mission Possible

There is very little difference in the business arena when it comes to leading a team, and companies that struggle with clear direction will struggle in many other areas as well. A clearly defined direction is not a vision statement. I can't believe the hours and money wasted identifying Vim's (vision, value, and mission) statements. I'm not at all opposed to the brainstorming that occurs to develop these, nor their intent (to get everyone on the same page and focused on a common goal). My opposition comes from the thousands of consultants lining their pockets helping the clients develop something they have no idea how to use. I should know; I used to be one of them until I saw how ineffective they were in communicating the real mission.

The final straw for me was when I asked a new client if he had completed one and he proudly said, "Sure," as he walked me to the filing cabinet and pulled it out. This is not execution by any stretch of the imagination. In almost any organization, there are three components: *the customer, the employee,* and *the finances.* Good direction clearly defines the goal for each of these three areas. You don't need proper verbiage in a paragraph called a mission statement to accomplish this. As a matter of fact, very few people can tell you what the company mission statement is anyway. But they can remember customer, employee, and money! So set goals around these three areas and give the employees clear focus by helping them find the rallying point. That is what good direction is about.

First, you develop a *mission*, not a mission statement, but a mission. What is the real purpose behind what this organization does? It should be short and concise. What describes the passion of what you're trying to accomplish?

From the mission, you create the GOST. In starting with the *G (Goal)*, that describes what the goal of the organization is? Then you move to the *O (Objective)*, a global measurement that is the gauge showing whether you are accomplishing the goal or not. You must use "if … then" logic to ensure you have enough objective measurements to ensure the goal is met. This is done by saying, "If xx and yy and zz, then we will inevitably accomplish the goal."

Once this is done, move on to the *S (Strategy)*, which are all of the strategies that must be deployed to ensure the objective is meeting the measurements you've established. Once this is complete, establish the *T (Tactic)* which is the measurement that shows that the strategies are being met. The uniqueness of this model is how everything must flow from the top down, providing clear direction and accountability that is communicated clearly through a single document.

This starts out at a functional level, beginning at the highest level of the organization. The board of directors develops its GOST, which then goes to the next level—the executive team, where they create their own GOST. However, the GO of the board become the ST of the executive team. Then the executive team GOST goes to the next level. The next level can be by function (department), organizational structure (i.e., additional profit centers or companies within the main business), or by management level. However the structure, the GOST continues to flow to each level by the GO becoming the ST for each subsequent level. An example by management level looks like this: executive ST is the GO for the middle manager, whose ST is the GO for the first line supervisors, and so on.

Conclusion

This model is the closest to a true democracy I've seen work inside a business. As is true with our democratic society, there are times for involvement and times to take orders. You don't put a committee together to put out a fire. Therefore, proper organizational structure, clearly defined roles, responsibilities, and expectations are all requirements for proper accountability.

Once a leader has a clear DCA model in place, it becomes his responsibility to use his coaching skills to ensure that the employees are getting proper feedback on a continual basis about their own individual development.

[Strategy 8]

The High-Performance Entrepreneur Has a Marketing Mindset

David P. Hale, PhD

> *Doing business without advertising is like winking at a girl in the dark.*
> *You know what you are doing, but nobody else does.*
> **Steuart Henderson Britt**

Good marketing is critical to the success of your business. Marketing has many dimensions, including market research, customer service, advertising, targeting, packaging, pricing, e-marketing, and others. Investing in a good marketing plan will generate excellent returns and be what propels your business in front of your target market.

What Is Marketing?

In plain and simple terms, marketing activities and strategies result in making products available that satisfy a customer need, while making profits for the companies that offer those products. That is it in a nutshell!

Marketing produces a win-win situation because:

- Customers have a product that meets their needs.

- Healthy profits are achieved for the company. (These profits allow the company to continue to do business in order to meet the needs of future customers.)

Stated another way, focusing on what the customer wants is essential to successful performance marketing efforts. This customer orientation must also be balanced with the company's objective of maintaining a profitable volume of sales in order for the company to continue to do business. Marketing is a creative, ever-changing orchestration of all the activities needed to accomplish both these objectives.

Meeting the Customer and Business Objectives

The American Marketing Association describes marketing as: "The process of planning and executing the conception, pricing, promotion, and distribution of ideas, goods, and services to create exchanges that satisfy individual and organizational objectives."

You see in the above definition that the process of marketing begins with discovering what products customers want to buy. Providing the features and quality customers want is a critical first step in marketing. You will be facing an uphill battle if you provide something you want to produce and then try to convince someone to buy it.

The marketing process continues with setting a price, letting potential customers know about your product, and making it available to them.

What to Include in Your Marketing

Marketing activities are numerous and varied because they basically include everything needed to get a product off the drawing board and into the hands of the customer. One look at the world of marketing shows that the broad field of marketing includes activities such as designing the product so it will be desirable to customers, using tools such as marketing research and pricing, promoting the product so people will know about it, using tools such as public relations, advertising, marketing communications, and interactions with the customer (through sales and distribution).

It is important to note that the field of marketing includes sales, but it also includes many other functions. Many people mistakenly think that marketing and sales are the same—they are not.

How Will Marketing Fit into Your Company?

Another way to describe marketing activities is to consider the big picture of how they fit in with the other business functions. Through marketing efforts, decisions are made and strategies are implemented concerning:

- What products (goods, services or ideas) will you be offering?
- Who will you sell to (the target market)?
- How will you sell it to them (how to inform potential customers of the offering, how to make the transaction, etc)?

Products are created through production efforts. Capital and operating funds are managed and tracked in the accounting-finance area, while the focus of the human resources area is employees and the policies concerning them. Often times, a marketing approach relies upon the coordination of several business areas to be successful. For example:

- The product might need some tweaking by the producer of the product to respond to customer complaints.

- The person who handles human resource issues might be asked to develop compensation plans that reward salespeople who build significant relationships that have tremendous potential, but are slow to close.

- Special payment plans might need to be implemented by the accounting staff to accommodate a variety of customer needs.

As a result, marketing usually crosses more departmental boundaries than other business functions do. Marketing requires the orchestration of everyone who plays a part in the common goal of pleasing the customer. For a small business owner who has no employees, this means that he/she needs to mentally tear down the walls between varied business functions and think holistically when it comes to marketing strategies.

These are the fundamentals of a true High-Performance Marketing Mindset:

- Producing what the customer wants should be the focus of business operations and planning.

- Creating profitable sales volume, not just sales volume, is a necessary goal.

- Coordinating between marketing activities and all other functions within a business that affect marketing efforts is a must.

Marketing Basics

To succeed, you the entrepreneur must attract and retain a growing base of satisfied customers. Marketing programs, though widely varied, are all aimed at convincing people to try out or keep using particular products or services. You should carefully plan your marketing strategies to keep your market presence strong.

Marketing is based on the importance of customers to a business and has two important principles:

- All company policies and activities should be directed toward satisfying customer needs.

- Profitable sales volume is more important than maximum sales volume.

To best use these principles, a small business should:

- Determine the needs of their customers through market research.
- Analyze their competitive advantages to develop a market strategy.
- Select specific markets to serve by target marketing.
- Determine how to satisfy customer needs by identifying a market mix.

Market Research

Successful marketing requires timely and relevant market information. An inexpensive research program, based on questionnaires given to current or prospective customers, can often uncover dissatisfaction or possible new products or services.

Market research will also identify trends that affect sales and profitability. Population shifts, legal developments, and the local economic situation should be monitored to quickly identify problems and opportunities. It is also important to keep up on your competitors' market strategies.

Marketing Strategy

A marketing strategy identifies customer groups that a particular business can better serve than its target competitors; it tailors product offerings, prices, distribution, promotional efforts, and services toward those segments. Ideally, the strategy should address unmet customer needs that offer adequate potential profitability. A good strategy helps a business focus on the target markets it can serve best.

Target Marketing

Owners of small businesses usually have limited resources to spend on marketing. Concentrating your efforts on one or a few key market segments—target marketing—gets the most return from small investments. There are two methods used to segment a market:

1. *Geographical segmentation:* Specializing in serving the needs of customers in a particular geographical area. For example, a neighborhood convenience store may send advertisements only to people living within one-half mile of the store.

2. *Customer segmentation:* Identifying those people most likely to buy the product or service and targeting those groups.

It is important to remember that the focus of marketing is people. If you are concentrating your efforts on your product or profit only, you will miss the mark. The term "target market" is used because that market—that group of people—is the bull's eye at which you aim all your marketing efforts.

So, do not forget that a market is people—people with common characteristics that set them apart as a group. The more statistics you have about a target market, the more precisely you can develop your strategy. Following are examples of market segments (or groups) and their characteristics:

- *Demographic Segment:* Measurable statistics such as age, income, occupation, etc.

- *Psychographic Segment:* Lifestyle preferences such as music lovers, city or urban dwellers, etc.

- *Use-based Segment:* Frequency of usage such as recreational drinking, traveling, etc.

- *Benefit Segment:* Desire to obtain the same product benefits such as luxury, thriftiness, comfort from food, etc.

- *Geographic Segment:* Location such as home address, business address, etc.

Here are examples of target segments that can be created using the above information:

- Women business owners between the ages of twenty-five and sixty earning more than $25,000 annually form a demographic segment.

- People who drive compact cars due to their fuel efficiency form a benefit segment.

Be careful not to confuse a geographic market segment with a place. The market is the people who live in the Sunbelt area, not the Sunbelt area. This is a common mistake made by business owners that causes them to lose a marketing focus on their customers.

Design Your Marketing Strategies with Your Target Market in Mind

The reason to be concerned with identifying a target market is that it makes strategies for designing, pricing, distributing, promoting, positioning, and improving your product, service, or idea easier, more effective, and more cost-effective.

For example, if research shows that a sturdy recyclable package with blue lettering appeals to your target market, and you are people oriented, you will likely choose that type of packaging. If, however, you are product or profit oriented—rather than people oriented—you might simply make the package out of plain Styrofoam because it protects the product (product oriented) or because it is cheap (profit oriented).

Here is another example: If you know your target market is twenty-four- to forty-nine-year-old men who like rhythm and blues, are frequent CD buyers, and live in urban neighborhoods, you can create an advertising message to appeal to those types of buyers. Additionally, you could buy spots on a specific radio station or TV show that appeals to this type of buyer, rather than buying general media time to cover all the bases. Makes sense, does it not?

Take a stab at your marketing strategy:

_____

_____

_____

_____

_____

Managing the Market Mix

Every marketing program contains four key components:

- Products and Services
- Promotion
- Distribution
- Pricing

Products and Services: Product strategies may include concentrating on a narrow product line, developing a highly specialized product or service, or providing a product-service package containing unusually high-quality service.

Promotion: Promotion strategies include advertising and direct customer interaction. Good salesmanship is essential for small businesses because of their limited ability to spend on advertising. Good telephone book advertising is also important. Direct mail is an effective, low-cost medium available to small business.

Pricing: The right price is crucial for maximizing total revenue. Generally, higher prices mean lower volume and vice versa; however, small businesses can often command higher prices because of their personalized service.

Distribution: The manufacturer and wholesaler must decide how to distribute their products. Working through established distributors or manufacturers' agents is generally easiest for small manufacturers. Small retailers should consider cost and traffic flow in site selection, especially since advertising and rent can be reciprocal: a low-cost, low-traffic location means spending more on advertising to build traffic.

These all combine into an overall marketing program.

The nature of the product or service is also important in making decisions. If purchases are based largely on impulse, then high-traffic and visibility are critical. On the other hand, location is less of a concern for products or services that customers are willing to go out of their way to find. The recent availability of highly segmented mailing lists, purchased from list brokers, magazines, or other companies, has enabled certain small businesses to operate from any location, yet serve national or international markets.

Marketing Performance

After implementing a marketing program, you must evaluate its performance. Every program should have performance standards to compare with actual results. Researching industry norms and past performances will help to develop appropriate standards.

You will need to audit your company's performance at least quarterly. The key questions are:

- Is the company doing all it can to be customer oriented?

- Do employees ensure the customers are satisfied and leave wanting to come back?

- Is it easy for the customer to find what he or she wants at a competitive price?

Market Research

What Is Marketing Research?

According to the American Marketing Association, marketing research is described as, "The systematic gathering, recording, and analyzing of data about problems relating to the marketing of goods and services."

Every small business owner/manager must ask the following questions to devise effective marketing strategies:

- Who are my customers and potential customers?
- What kind of people are they?
- Where do they live?
- What can and will they buy?
- Am I offering the kinds of goods or services they want at the best place, at the best time, and in the right amounts?
- Are my prices consistent with what buyers view as the product's value?
- Are my promotional programs working?
- What do customers think of my business?
- How does my business compare with my competitors?

Marketing research is not a perfect science. It deals with people and their constantly changing feelings and behaviors, which are influenced by countless subjective factors. To conduct marketing research, you must gather facts and opinions in an orderly, objective way to find out what people want to buy, not just what you want to sell them.

Why Do I Need to Do This?

It is impossible to sell products or services that customers do not want. Trying to do so is like an Eskimo trying to sell ice cream in the middle of the winter in Alaska. Who will buy it? Learning what customers want and how to present it attractively drives the need for marketing research. Small businesses have an edge over larger concerns in this regard. Large businesses must hire experts to study the mass market, while small-scale entrepreneurs are close to their customers and can learn much more quickly about their buying habits. Small business owners have a sense their customers' needs from years of experience, but this informal information may not be timely or relevant to the current market.

Marketing research focuses and organizes marketing information. It ensures that such information is timely and permits entrepreneurs to:

- Reduce business risks
- Spot current and upcoming problems in the current market
- Identify sales opportunities
- Develop plans of action

How Do I Do This?

Without being aware of it, most business owners do market research every day. So, you are probably experienced, and you don't even know it. Analyzing returned items, asking former customers why they've switched, and looking at competitor's prices are all examples of such research. Formal marketing research simply makes this familiar process orderly. It provides a framework to organize market information.

Market Research—The Process

Market research, like other components of marketing such as advertising, can be quite simple or very complex. You might conduct simple market research such as including a questionnaire in your customer bills to gather demographic information about your customers. On the more complex side, you might engage a professional market research firm to conduct primary research to aid you in developing a marketing strategy to launch a new product.

Regardless of the simplicity or complexity of your marketing research project, you will benefit by reviewing the following seven stages in the market research process.

Stage One: Define Marketing Problems and Opportunities

The market research process begins with identifying and defining the problems and opportunities that exist for your business, such as:

- Launching a new product, service, or business
- Low awareness of your company and its products or services
- Low utilization of your company's products or services (the market is familiar with your company, but still is not doing business with you)
- A poor company image and reputation
- Problems with distribution—your goods and services are not reaching the buying public in a timely manner

What's Your Problem?

The first stage of the research process, defining the problem or opportunity, is often overlooked—but it is crucial. The root cause of the problem is harder to identify than its obvious manifestations; for example, a decline in sales is a problem, but its underlying cause is what must be corrected. To define the problem, list every factor that may have influenced it, then eliminate any that cannot be measured. Examine this list while conducting research to see if any factors ought to be added, but do not let it unduly influence data collection.

Problem: _____

_____

_____

_____

Contributing Factor(s):

1. _____
2. _____
3. _____
4. _____
5. _____
6. _____

Stage Two: Develop Objectives, Timetables, and Budget

Objective: With a marketing problem or opportunity defined, the next step is to set objectives for your market research operations. Your objective might be to explore the nature of a problem so you may further define it, or perhaps it is to determine how many people will buy your product packaged in a certain way and offered at a certain price. Your objective might even be to test possible cause and effect relationships. For example, if you lower your price by 10 percent, what increased sales volume should you expect? What impact will this strategy have on your profit?

Identify your objective:

_____

_____

_____

_____

Timetables: Prepare a detailed, realistic timeframe to complete all steps of the market research process. If your business operates in cycles, establish target dates that will allow the best accessibility to your market. For example, a holiday greeting card business may want to conduct research before or around the holiday season buying period, when their customers are most likely to be thinking about their purchases.

Identify your timetable:

_____

_____

_____

_____

Budget: How much money are you willing to invest in your market research? How much can you afford? Your market research budget is a portion of your overall marketing budget. A popular method with small business owners to establish a marketing budget is to allocate a percentage of gross sales for the previous year. This usually amounts to about 2 percent for an existing business. However, if you are planning on launching a new product or business, you may want to increase your budget figure to as much as 10 percent of your expected gross sales. Other methods used by small businesses include analyzing and estimating the competition's budget and calculating your cost of marketing per sale.

Identify your market research budget:

_____

_____

_____

_____

Stage Three: Determine the Research Types, Methods, and Techniques You Will Use

There are two types of research: *primary research* or original information gathered for a specific purpose, and *secondary research* or information that already exists somewhere. Both types of research have a number of activities and methods of conducting associated with them. Secondary research is usually faster and less expensive to obtain than primary research. Gathering secondary research may be as simple as making a trip to your local library or business information center or browsing the Internet.

Primary Research

Primary research can be as simple as asking customers or suppliers how they feel about a business or as complex as surveys conducted by professional marketing research firms. Direct mail questionnaires, telephone surveys, experiments, panel studies, test marketing, and behavior observation are all examples of primary research.

Primary research is often divided into reactive and non-reactive research. Non-reactive primary research observes how real people behave in real market situations without influencing that behavior even accidentally. Reactive research, including surveys, interviews, and questionnaires, is best left to marketing professionals, as they can usually get more objective and sophisticated results.

Those who cannot afford high-priced marketing research services should consider asking nearby college or university business schools for help.

Secondary Research

Secondary research exploits published sources like surveys, books, and magazines and applies or rearranges the information in them to bear on the problem or opportunity at hand. A tire sales business owner might guess that present retail sales of tires are strongly correlated with sales of new cars three years ago. To test this idea, it is easy to compare new car sales records with replacement tire sales three years later. Done over a range of recent years, this should prove or disprove the hypothesis and help marketing efforts tremendously.

Localized figures tend to provide better information as local conditions might buck national trends. Newspapers and other local media are often quite helpful. Your local chamber of commerce is a goldmine of information.

There are many sources of secondary research material. It can be found in libraries, colleges, trade, and general business publications, and newspapers. Trade associations and government agencies are rich sources of information—*Gales Directory* is available at most public library.

Sources of Secondary Research

- ASAE Directory of Associations Online—www.asaecenter.org/index.cfm
- Ask a Librarian—U.S. Library of Congress—www.loc.gov/rr/askalib
- Bureau of Labor Statistics—www.stats.bls.gov
- Business Research Lab—www.busreslab.com/evaluhd.htm
- Center for Business Women's Research—www.womensbusinessresearch.org

- Economic Statistics and Research—www.sba.gov/advo/research
- Federal Statistics—www.fedstats.gov
- Internet Public Library—www.ipl.org
- Population and Demography Resources—www.pstc.brown.edu

Identify what research types, methods, and techniques you will use:

_____

_____

_____

_____

Stage Four: Design Research Instruments

The most common research instrument is the questionnaire. Keep these high-performance tips in mind when designing your market research questionnaire.

- Keep it simple. Include instructions for answering all questions on the survey.
- Begin the survey with general questions and move toward more specific questions.
- Keep each question brief.
- If the questionnaire is completed by the respondent and not by an interviewer or survey staff member, remember to design a questionnaire that is graphically pleasing and easy to read.
- Pre-test the questionnaire. Before taking the survey to the printer, ask a few people such as regular customers, colleagues, friends, or employees to complete the survey. Ask them for feedback on the survey's style, simplicity, and their perception of its purpose.
- Mix the form of the questions. Use scales, rankings, open-end questions, and closed-end questions for different sections of the questionnaire. The form or way a question is asked may influence the answer given. Basically, there are two question forms: closed-end questions and open-end questions.

Closed-end questions. Respondents choose from possible answers included on the questionnaire. Types of closed-end questions include:

- Multiple-choice questions that offer respondents the ability to answer "yes" or "no" or choose from a list of several answer choices.

- Scales refer to questions that ask respondents to rank their answers or measure their answer at a particular point on a scale. For example, a respondent may have the choice to rank their feelings toward a particular statement. The scale may range from "Strongly Disagree," "Disagree," and "Indifferent" to "Agree" and "Strongly Agree."

Open-end questions. Respondents answer questions in their own words. Completely unstructured questions allow respondents to answer any way they choose. Types of open-end questions include:

- Word association questions ask respondents to state the first word that comes to mind when a particular word is mentioned.

- Sentence, story, or picture completion questions ask respondents to complete partial sentences, stories, or pictures in their own words. For example, a question for commuters might read, "My daily commute between home and office is _____ miles and takes me an average of _____ minutes. I use the following mode of transportation: _____."

Stage Five: Collect Data

To help you obtain clear, unbiased, and reliable results, collect the data under the direction of experienced researchers. Before beginning the collection of data, it is important to train, educate, and supervise your research staff. An untrained staff person conducting primary research will lead to interviewer bias.

Stick to the objectives and rules associated with the methods and techniques you have set in stages two and three. Try to be as scientific as possible in gathering your information.

Stage Six: Organize and Analyze the Data

Once your data has been collected, it needs to be cleaned. Cleaning research data involves editing, coding, and tabulating results. To make this step easier, start with a simply designed research instrument or questionnaire.

Following are some helpful tips for organizing and analyzing your data:

- Look for relevant data that focuses on your immediate market needs.

- Rely on subjective information only as support for more general findings of objective research.

- Analyze for consistency by comparing the results of different methods of your data collection. For example, are the market demographics provided to you from the local media outlet consistent with your survey results?

- Quantify your results; look for common opinions that may be counted together.

- Read between the lines. For example, combine U.S. Census Bureau statistics on median income levels for a given location and the number of homeowners versus renters in the area.

Stage Seven: Present and Use Market Research Findings

Once marketing information about your target market, competition, and environment is collected and analyzed, present it in an organized manner to the decision makers of your business. If this is yourself, you may want to report your findings in the market analysis section of your business plan. In addition, you may want to familiarize your sales and marketing departments (if you have them already) with the data or conduct a company-wide informational training seminar using the information. In summary, the resulting data was created to help guide your business decisions, so it needs to be readily accessible to the decision makers.

15 Sure-Fire Ideas for Promoting Your Business

Every successful company uses some sort of promotion to influence certain audiences—usually customers or prospects—by informing or persuading them. Reasons for promoting a business include: increasing visibility, adding credibility to you or your company, enhancing or improving your image, and bringing in new business. The following cost-effective, easy-to-execute ideas have the power to increase sales in a way conventional advertising cannot. The key is to find the methods that are appropriate for your business, marketplace, and professional style.

1. Contests. For example, a cookware store decided to sponsor cooking contests. After sending out a press release announcing a competition for the best cookie or chocolate cake, a mailing went out to the store's customers soliciting entries. Food editors, professional chefs, and cooking teachers were invited to be judges. Both the winners and the winning recipes were publicized.

2. Newsletters or Blogs. Another good way to promote, particularly for brokers, banks, and business consultants, is through newsletters. They demonstrate how much you know about your field in a low-key, informative way. They help keep your company high in the consciousness of your prospects. Today, many businesses have blogs that are updated on a daily basis. You can relate the article content to your products and services. There is no better way to show your expertise than your published word.

3. Demonstrations. Demonstrations are an option to attract people to your place of business, show them how to best use your product, and establish your credibility. For example, a wholesale fish outlet holds cooking demonstrations twice a week, featuring a different restaurant chef each time, and attracting substantial crowds, and handing out recipe cards are even given out. Another example: some grocery stores prepare food items using products within the store and give away samples.

4. Seminars. Often more appropriate for business-to-business marketing, seminars are the commercial side of demonstrations. If you hold a seminar, follow these rules for success:

- Schedule the event at a time convenient to most attendees.
- Be specific in the invitation about when the event begins and ends, who will be there, and what the agenda is.
- Follow up the invitations with personal phone calls.
- Charge for the seminar to give it a higher perceived value.
- Follow up after the event to get people's reactions.

5. Premiums. Also called an advertising specialty, a premium is a gift of some kind that reminds your customer of you and your service. There are thousands from which to choose: key chains, coffee mugs, refrigerator magnets, baseball caps, paperweights—just about anything that can be engraved, imprinted, silk-screened, or embroidered with your company name and phone number. Make the item unique to your business.

6. Speeches. Depending on your topic and market, you might want to speak before chambers of commerce, trade associations, parent groups, senior citizens, or other local organizations.

7. Articles. Another possibility is to write an article for a trade journal, reprint it, and mail it off to your friends, customers, and prospects. This positions you as an expert and is a particularly good way to promote a consulting business.

8. Bonuses. If you have a restaurant, give away a glass of wine with dinner to introduce a new menu. If you sell to retailers, give them a display fixture with the order of a gross. If you sell office supplies, give away a new pen with a size-able purchase. If you are in the cosmetics business, offer customers a free sample blusher when they buy mascara and lipstick. When using this method, you can up-sell complimentary products or services at a discount—commonly referred to as add-ons.

9. Coupons. For best results, the price break should be significant—at least 15 percent. This is one of the least expensive ways to develop new trade and an excellent tool for evaluating advertising. However, one theory holds that coupons draw people who only buy discount and never become regular customers, so be sure to monitor the results.

10. Donations. Donating your product or service to a charitable cause often results in positive exposure to community leaders, charity board members, PTAs, and civic groups. While consumer products are desired most, many organizations also look for donations of professional service time. If you have a restaurant or a large meeting facility, consider hosting an event for a charitable organization. This works best if volunteers for that charity are potential customers.

11. Samples. No matter what you do to promote your business, giving potential customers a sample is an excellent way to attract attention and make a positive impression. In many cases, it makes just as much sense to spend your marketing and advertising dollars on giving out your own products instead of buying adver-tisements, especially if cash is tight. The key is to give samples to the audience you want to reach (e.g., software packages to computer user groups or nutritious snacks to health-oriented consumers). In the food arena, where one taste is worth a thousand words, firms now exist that test-market new products for large and small companies alike through in-store demonstrations. A good demonstration company not only keeps track of how much of your product was given away, but also submits detailed reports on what people said about the product and how much of it was purchased.

12. Free Trials. If your product is too big or expensive to give away outright, why not offer a free trial to qualified customers. Try shipping it out to prospects with no strings attached. Most people will appreciate the opportunity to try the product, and hopefully many will like it enough to buy it.

13. Free Services. If you cannot afford to give away products, offering your services as a way of generating new business can also pay off. For example, if you own a retail clothing business, send out a flyer offering customers a free fashion consultation to draw them into the store.

14. Special Benefits, Rates, or Notices. Smart organizations go out of their way to make customers feel important and appreciated. Frequent flyer clubs are the most pervasive example of loyalty-building benefits for customers only; this method has been adapted by many kinds of businesses. Most software companies sell program updates to customers at discounted prices, and advance notices about sales, changes, or opportunities can help cement customer ties.

15. Say Thanks. One of the best ways to let customers know you value their business and encourage their continued patronage is also one of the easiest. It boils down to saying thank you in letters, mailers, surveys, statement stuffers, receipts, invoices, and in person. You may also do this by holding a customer loyalty day.

High-Performance Marketing Programs You Can Implement in a Week

Ideas about marketing have changed dramatically during the past several years. In contrast to the 1980s approach of creating aggressive strategies to compel sales, the new style focuses on developing a service-oriented business dedicated to solving customers' problems.

It is sometimes called customer-centered marketing, and it is not as simple as it sounds. For one thing, providing customers with real solutions requires a good deal of research and insight. Yet businesses too often adopt a quick-fix response convenient for them and call it customer centered. For example, twenty-four-hour service lines are easily set up and seem customer focused, but research might show that what a firm's customers actually need is a toll-free fax line for describing operating problems to technicians. In short, mere lip service to customer support is not enough. Companies must truly look beyond their internal considerations to focus squarely on their target audience.

The other challenge in customer-centered marketing is that it must also be competition centered. The only way to pull customers from your competition is to offer a better mouse trap. That is, show them you offer a better solution. You must exploit new markets or new opportunities your competition has not ventured into. You must remain vigilant of your competition.

Additionally, many startups are simply not market oriented. A key sign that problems exist is if the company does not have an established marketing plan. Many companies find themselves spending money on marketing only when the bottom has fallen out and there are no sales.

All told, the way to success is clear. Go the extra mile to give your customers high-quality, competitive products and services. Spend money to make money. Work to attract and, more importantly, retain your customers with every well-produced marketing device appropriate to your business: newspaper and Yellow Pages ads, brochures, direct mail, TV and radio spots, newsletters, telemarketing, public relations, community sponsorships, trade shows, billboards, special events, and more.

Follow Up on Every Sale

Regularly evaluate all your transactions with customers to monitor the quality of your products and services, and ask customers how you can improve. Fortunately, you can do this easily, again using a questionnaire.

Keep questionnaires short and make sure each question concerns only one issue (e.g., "Was the delivery crew prompt and courteous?" is two questions, not one). In addition, try to avoid yes/no questions and offer check-off ratings in no more than four questions, ensuring that customers are putting their ideas into short answers more often than mechanically checking boxes.

To keep the questionnaire well focused and concise, stick to the big issues or the critical points. Begin constructing your questionnaire by writing out every potential question you can think of, then narrow it down to the six to twelve that matter most.

An even more important part of follow-up than a questionnaire is to thank customers for their business—which you can do in a short note—and put their names on a mailing list. Then send them any of a variety of useful mailers: notices of new products or services, information about products and services related to recent purchases, sales notices, special promotions, and newsletters.

Whatever else you may include as part of your marketing plan, do not skimp on follow-up, for the follow-up is the key to keeping your customers.

Use Your Database to Write Customers a Personal Letter

Database marketing is aimed at keeping customers, not making a sale. The underlying technique is to use database records of customers' latest purchases as well as frequency and amount of past purchases, to create targeted mailers that let you stay in touch with your customers.

Take the time to concentrate on customers individually by writing them letters personally tailored to their specific situation. Mention that you will phone in a week to follow up on the specific concern. And, add a handwritten P.S. recapping your main message.

Build Awareness through Sweepstakes or Contests

Sweepstakes and contests provide exciting ways to build awareness of your products, services, and company, as well as produce the goodwill that giveaways naturally inspire. Whether entrants will win a free lunch at your restaurant or a free week in Paris (perhaps co-sponsored by a local travel agent), you must check the legalities with your lawyer before you start.

Then plan your promotion step by step, from how customers will enter and how entries will be handled to whether you will award prizes below the grand-prize category. For example, will everyone win something just for entering?

Finally, create an entry form and eye-catching collection box and advertise with flyers, mailers, banners, store signs, newspaper ads, or radio spots. If you will collect entries in your store, place the box at the back of the premises so everybody must pass through your merchandise to reach it.

Afterward, generate publicity about the winners and display photocopies of all resulting news stories at your business.

Be Creative with Telephone-Hold Marketing

In most businesses, callers will at some point be placed on hold; play a telephone-hold audiotape that, over background music, talks about your products, services, or even your company itself. Besides helping the time pass faster, tapes can answer callers' questions and even inform them of products or services they need but didn't know you provide.

To find a company to produce your telephone-hold tape, check the Yellow Pages and Internet under "Telecommunications—Telephone Equipment, Services, and Systems." Most firms provide everything you need—produced tape, hookups, and phone equipment—for a monthly fee.

Sell with Store and Vehicle Signs

Use interior signs if you have a store location to tell customers about the goods and services you offer, such as free delivery, free alterations, or free trials. If you stock a specialty line, like environmentally-safe products, point it out. If you have just received merchandise with a high-demand feature, let customers know.

Signs also provide an easy way to answer customers' most commonly-asked questions. Post explanatory labels to help customers differentiate among various models. Write out shelf signs describing special features that make products outstanding values or unique in their field, or telling customers where to find accessories.

You can also place magnetic or decal signs on your vehicle advertising your business. This is inexpensive and a great way to get your business name out there. Use signs, in short, to tout your company's competitive advantages and to make shopping easier, more informative, and more motivating for your customers.

Act Now to Extend Your Seasonal Sales

Is your business seasonal? If so, utilize year-round marketing to improve your sales. Before the season, stimulate repeat sales by sending coupons to current customers for upcoming purchases or offering special deals on early orders. After the season, use follow-up mailings or phone calls to stay in touch with customers and encourage their loyalty. Maintain interest with an end-of-season or off-season sale of leftover merchandise.

In the longer term, consider a second-season business or product line that would be both a logical extension of your current operation and appeal to your customers. A holiday fruitcake company, for example, might branch out into year-round baked goods, or a ski shop into camping gear. If you are a retail firm, expand not your season but your customer base by adding a catalog or direct-mail wholesale operation.

To sum up, marketing is a 365-days-a-year job; it demands persistent attention in satisfying customers' needs. Equally important, it requires a constant program of efforts to develop your customer base and stimulate sales—a program initiated and implemented most effectively by putting your own twist on direct, hard-working, tried-and-true ideas such as the six described in this section. It does not take novelty or large sums of money to succeed in marketing; first and foremost, it takes action.

E-Marketing

E-mail marketing is one of the most effective ways to keep in touch with customers. It is generally cost-effective, and if done properly, can help build brand awareness and loyalty. At a typical cost of only a few cents per message, it is a bargain compared to traditional direct mail at a dollar or more per piece. In addition, response rates on e-mail marketing are strong, ranging from 5 to 35 percent depending on the industry and format. Response rates for traditional mail averages in the 1 to 3 percent range.

One of the benefits of e-mail marketing is the demographic information that customers provide when signing up for your e-mail newsletter. Discovering who your customers really are—age, gender, income, and special interests, for example—can help you target your products and services to their needs.

Points to consider when creating your e-mail newsletter:

- *HTML versus Plain Text:* Response rates for HTML newsletters are generally far higher than plain text, and graphics and colors tend to make the publications look a lot more professional. The downside is that HTML e-mail is slower to download, and some e-mail providers may screen out HTML e-mail.

- *Provide incentive to subscribe:* To get customers to sign up for your newsletter, advertise the benefits of receiving your newsletter, such as helpful tips, informative content, or early notification of special offers or campaigns, and coupons.

- *Do not just sell:* Many studies suggest that e-mail newsletters are read far more carefully when they offer information that is useful to the customers' lives rather than merely selling products and services. Helpful tips, engaging content, and humor are often expected to accompany e-mail newsletters.

- *Limit questions:* As each demographic question you ask may reduce the number of customers signing up, it is best to limit the amount of information you solicit or give customers the option of skipping the questionnaire.

Check out www.hiperwebsolutions.com for offers on e-marketing services and tools.

Conclusion

Without proper marketing and advertisement, how will your customers know you exist? By adopting a marketing mindset, not only will you get your company name out in front of your target market, but you will also begin to think from a marketing perspective.

By continually thinking from a marketing point of view, you will build brand awareness around your business through sales, newsletters, Web site offers, coupons, and database targeting.

[Strategy 9]

The High-Performance Entrepreneur Writes a Marketing Plan

David P. Hale, PhD

> *You have to know the rules of the game. And then you*
> *need to play better than anyone else.*
> **Albert Einstein**

A sound marketing plan is the key to the success of your business. It should include your market research, location, the customer group you plan to or have been targeting, competition, positioning, your product or service you are selling, pricing, advertising, and promotion.

Effective marketing, planning, and promotion begin with current information about the marketplace. Specifically, the marketplace you plan on targeting. So, at this point, you must begin to play detective in order to uncover the marketplace intelligence you need. To start, visit the libraries in your area, talk to past and prospective customers, study the advertising of other businesses in your community, and consult with any relevant industry associations. This interactive strategy will help you assess your marketing strengths and weaknesses.

To guide you on your search, use the below topics to find the information and facts you need to answer when writing your formal marketing plan.

1. Define your business:

- Your product or service
- Your geographic marketing area—neighborhood, regional, or national
- Your competition
- How you differ from the competition—what makes you special
- Your price
- The competition's promotion methods

- Your promotion methods
- Your distribution methods or business location

2. Define your customers:

- Who is your current customer base (age, sex, income, and neighborhood)?
- How do your customers learn about your product or service—advertising, direct mail, word of mouth, Yellow Pages, Internet?
- What patterns or habits do your customers and potential customers share (i.e., where they shop, what they read, watch, and listen to)?
- What qualities do your customers value most about your product or service, such as selection, convenience, service, reliability, availability, and affordability?
- What qualities do your customers like least about your product or service? Can they be adjusted to serve your customers better?
- Which prospective customers are you currently not reaching?

3. Define your plan and budget:

- Previous marketing methods you have used to communicate to your customers
- Methods that have been most effective
- Cost compared to sales
- Cost per customer
- Possible future marketing methods to attract new customers
- Percentage of profits you can allocate to your marketing campaign
- Marketing tools you can implement within your budget—newspaper, magazine, Yellow Pages, radio or television advertising, direct mail, telemarketing, and public relations activities such as community involvement, sponsorship, Internet marketing, or press releases
- Methods of testing your marketing ideas
- Methods for measuring results of your marketing campaign
- The marketing tool you can implement immediately

The final component in your marketing plan should be your overall promotional objectives: to communicate your message, create an awareness of your product or service, motivate customers to buy and increase sales, or other specific targets. Objectives make it easier to design an effective campaign and help you keep that campaign on the right track. Once you have defined your objectives, it is easier to choose the method that will be most effective.

Writing Your Marketing Plan

Marketing Plan Components:

Executive Summary
Situation Analysis
Competitor and Issues Analysis
Marketing Objectives and Strategy
Strategy and Implementation

1. Executive Summary

The Executive Summary section of your marketing plan allows you to introduce your company and explain the major points of your plan. For the people who lack the time and interest to read your entire marketing plan, the Executive Summary is for them.

Since the Executive Summary is an encapsulated version of the major points of your entire plan, you will actually write it after completing everything else. Some of the key points to cover are:

   a. **Introduce your company by briefly describing the nature of your business and the products or services you offer.**

   • If your business is already running, explain how long you have been in business and how long you have been at your current location. Describe your business activities including sales and customers. Highlight your accomplishments and successes.

   • If your business is not yet in operation, describe the experience and training you have that qualifies you to operate this type of business. Include similar information for business partners or key managers of the company.

b. **State your founding philosophy—often called a mission statement—and company objectives.**

- Mission statements are relatively abstract, such as "to provide quality day care for children."

- Company objectives are more specific, such as "to be the child-care provider of choice in the Tri-County area and to increase enrollment by 25 percent in twelve months." Your objectives are basically how you will carry out your mission statement.

c. **Introduce your management team. (In many cases, this may be only you occupying many positions!)**

- Describe the organizational structure of your business. Is it a sole proprietorship, partnership, or corporation?

- List the key management personnel. Include copies of their resumes in the supporting documents section.

- Disclose management salaries and ownership, management assistance and training needs, and supporting professionals (such as a bookkeeper or lawyer).

- List the board of directors.

d. **Close the Executive Summary with a brief statement of the main marketing objectives and strategies contained in the plan.**

2. Situation Analysis

In the Situation Analysis section, you will provide information about your location, target market, and competitive environment. You will briefly describe the competitive environment and key issues your company faces in this section. You will later provide more detail in the Competitor and Issue Analysis section.

a. Location

Describe your current or planned business location.

- If you do not yet have a business location, name areas or properties under consideration and the criteria you will use in selecting a location. Consider customer proximity, parking availability, accessibility by public transportation, employee availability, inventory storage and movement, compliance with federal, state, and local laws and codes (such as those for zoning, safety, or health), security, and site expansion potential.

- List any negative aspects of your location that would affect sales (such as a lack of sufficient parking) and try to list solutions for such problems. Remember that no location is perfect; try to turn every negative around and make it a positive.

- Describe any plans for the future expansion of your business. Do you intend to move? Will you offer additional goods or services as you grow? Will you hire employees?

- If you offer or plan to offer a service or product in a manner that does not require customers to visit a location, include a description of how you and your customers will meet or interact and how services and products will be exchanged. This may be the case if your product is a consulting service you provide from home or at a client location. In addition, if your products are offered through catalog sales or on the Internet, you would describe how your services and/or products would be exchanged with customers.

b. Target Market Description

Critical to your success in marketing any product is aiming all your marketing efforts at a target market. Planning your marketing strategy without knowing to whom you are trying to appeal is like planning a party without knowing anything about the people attending.

- Describe the size of your target market. Remember, a market is people with something in common, not a place, or a thing. Be specific and include statistics about the size of your target market. Include information on whether the size of your target marketing is growing, shrinking, or staying the same. If the size of your target market is changing, explain why.

- Describe your target market in the following terms:

  o Characteristics they share such as age, income level, sex, race, number of children, marital status, where they live, etc.

  o Habits or hobbies they exhibit. For example, your target audience may tend to be workaholics, which makes them good candidates for meals delivered to their homes or offices.

  o Wants and needs they have and how your product fulfills them. For example, most single, working mothers often need affordable, quality daycare for children.

- Describe your market's buying habits. For example, how do they spend their disposable income? When do they buy? How much? How often?

Note: You may have more than one target market. If so, identify your primary market—the customers who buy your products or services most often. Then, include secondary groups if you feel they will provide significant business. For each group, you must identify their characteristics, needs, etc. because you will most likely change your marketing strategy accordingly.

3. Competitor and Issues Analysis

The purpose of the Competitor and Issues Analysis section of your marketing plan is to explain in detail the external challenges and opportunities your business may face. Even though preparation of the analysis will take time, it will be worth it. You can benefit in a number of ways.

Benefits of Preparing a Competitor and Issues Analysis

- You will discover your company's competitive advantage—the reason customers do business with you instead of your competition. Then you will be able to *communicate* your competitive advantage effectively to win potential customers.

- Analyzing current issues and your competitors' offerings may spur ideas for innovative improvements to your product offerings.

- You might find that there are some categories of customers whose needs are not being met. For example, if you plan to prepare and deliver gourmet meals, you may discover that a particular part of town is not currently being served. If you can satisfy unmet needs, you will develop a market "niche."

- By observing the actions of your competitors, you might learn more about your market. For example, does a successful competitor offer reduced prices during a particular season? If so, what might that tell you about your market's spending habits?

- If you find that your market is saturated with capable competitors, you can avoid the costly mistake of starting a business without adequate demand. You can then redirect your efforts toward something that will pay off instead. (For example, your research may tell you that there's an ample number of thriving gourmet meal services in your targeted market area already.)

What to Address in Your Competitor Analysis

- **Names of competitors**. At first glance, this may seem like an exercise in list-making. Obviously, if you sell ice cream by the cone, your competitors include other ice cream vendors. However, you are also competing with other dessert treats offered by grocery stores as well as other items competing for consumers' discretionary funds. So, list *all* of your competitors and include information on any that might enter the market during the next year.

- **Summary of each competitor's products**. This summary should also include their location, quality, advertising, staff, distribution methods, promotional strategies, customer service, etc.

- **Competitors' strengths and weaknesses**. It is important to see your competitors' strengths and weaknesses from your *customer's viewpoint*, not yours. List their strengths and weaknesses. State how you will capitalize on their weaknesses and meet the challenges represented by their strengths.

- **Competitors' strategies and objectives**. This information might be easily obtained by getting a copy of their annual report. However, you will probably need to do some detective work or conduct an analysis of many information sources to understand competitors' strategies and objectives.

- **Strength of the market**. Is the market for your product growing sufficiently so there are plenty of customers for all market players? Or, is the market so tight you are selling primarily to your competitors' customers? (If so, you need to have a strong competitive advantage.)

Ideas for Gathering Competitive Information

- **Internet**. One of your most powerful tools. Google is wonderful, isn't it?

- **Personal visits**. If possible, visit your competitors' locations. Observe how employees interact with customers. What do their premises look like? How are their products displayed? Priced?

- **Talk to customers**. Your sales staff is in regular contact with customers and prospects. Your competition is also in contact with these people. Learn what your customers and prospects are saying about your competitors—and about you, too!

- **Competitors' ads**. Analyze competitors' ads to gain information about their target audience, market position, product features, benefits, prices, etc.

- **Speeches or presentations**. Attend speeches or presentations made by representatives of your competitors.
- **Trade show displays.** View your competitor's display with a critical eye and from a potential customer's point of view. What does their display "say" about the company? Even observing *which* trade shows or industry events competitors attend provides information on their marketing strategy and target market.
- **Written sources:**
  o General business publications
  o Marketing and advertising publications
  o Local newspapers and business journals
  o Industry and trade association publications
  o Industry research and surveys
  o Computer databases (available at many public libraries)
  o Annual reports
  o Yellow Pages

Hint: Create a file for each competitor. As you run across things like their marketing literature, tips from sales people or customers about them, or articles that mention them, place it in their file. Then, when you are ready to conduct or update your competitor analysis, you will already have some relevant resources.

What to Address in Your Issue Analysis

Your business will face obstacles to success in addition to those posed by the competition. Half the battle of overcoming these external obstacles is understanding them. And half the key to benefiting from "lucky breaks" is being on top of developments and events that can be used to your advantage.

1. **Threats and Opportunities (from outside)**. Identify, and rank by order of importance, any threats or opportunities your business may face from *outside influences*. Threats and opportunities come from a variety of sources including:

- The economic outlook of your market's economy. Are you starting your business in a healthy economy? If not, can your product still thrive?
- Product innovations. How will changes made to the products of your competitors affect you? What's happening with products that are "com-

plementary" to yours? (If you write software that runs on Windows, Dell PCs would be "complementary products" to you.)

- Technological advancements. What changes in technology will impact you?

- Environmental issues. Is your product earth-friendly?

- Government regulations. What impact does complying with government regulations have on your business? Is there any pending legislation that may impact you?

- Barriers to market entry. Are there high or low barriers to market entry in your field? What would it take for a competitor to start a business in your field? Could a competitor start up overnight (low barrier) or does your business require special knowledge, expensive machinery, etc. (high barrier)?

2. **Strengths and Weaknesses (inside your company)**. Identify *internal* strengths and weaknesses of your company. For example, your education, experience, and reputation in your area of expertise are most likely a strength. A weakness if you plan to have employees might be a lack of supervisory experience.

Summarize the Main Issues in an Issues Statement

Finally, determine which issues are most significant and integrate them into an Issues Statement. Use your carefully researched Issues Statement as you set your marketing objectives and strategy.

Here's an example of an issues statement:

"While there are few entry barriers in offering public relations counseling to small business owners (a telephone and computer are all that's required), the forty years combined experience of the partners of HiPer Solutions is its competitive advantage. No other coaching agency in the area HiPer serves offers a comparable depth of experience.

A professional manager is being recruited to compensate for the owner's lack of experience and interest in supervising employees. This person should be in place by August."

4. Marketing Objectives and Strategies

a. **Meeting marketing objectives should lead to sales.** (If not, you need to set different marketing objectives.) They should:

- Be clear
- Be measurable
- Have an identified date to achieve success

Examples of marketing objectives follow:

- Increase product awareness among the target audience by 30 percent in one year.
- Inform target audience about features and benefits of our product and its competitive advantage, leading to a 10 percent increase in sales in one year.
- Decrease or remove potential customers' resistance to buying our product, leading to a 20 percent increase in sales that are closed in six months or less.

If you have multiple objectives, make sure they are consistent and not in conflict with each other. Also, be sure that the remainder of your marketing plan components—the marketing strategy, budget, action programs, controls and measures, etc.—support your marketing objectives.

Setting your marketing objectives and finalizing the remaining components of your marketing plan may serve as a reality check: Do you have the resources necessary to accomplish your objectives?

b. **Strategize with the four Ps.**

The *Marketing Strategy* section of your plan outlines your game plan to achieve your marketing objectives. It is, essentially, the heart of the marketing plan. The marketing strategy section should include information about:

- Product—your product(s) and services
- Price—what you will charge customers for products and services
- Promotion—how you will promote or create awareness of your product in the marketplace
- Place (distribution)—how you will bring your product(s) together with your customers

Brief explanations of what should be included in the marketing strategy section of your marketing plan pertaining to the four Ps appear below.

Product Description

A product can be a physical item, a service, or an idea.

- Describe in detail your products or services in terms of the features and benefits they offer customers.
- Describe what you need to *have* or *do* to provide your product or service (how it is produced).

Pricing

List the price of your products and describe your pricing strategy, along with listing price *ranges* for product lines. For example, if your product is a line of cosmetics, include information in this strategy section about your lipsticks "ranging in price from $5.00 to $15.00 per item" rather than a detailed product price list.

Describe any price flexibility or negotiating room, as is common with large purchases such as houses or cars. Outline any discounts you offer for long-term customers, bulk purchases, or prompt payment. Also, include the terms of sale, such as "net due in 30 days," extended payment plans, and whether you accept credit cards.

Promotion Plan

A promotion plan describes the tools or tactics used to accomplish your marketing objectives.

If your marketing objective is:	Then tools or tactics might be:
Create awareness of baby care products among mothers of newborns.	<ul><li>Advertise in baby care or motherhood magazines.</li><li>Distribute product samples to obstetricians.</li><li>Offer free baby care seminars to expectant mothers.</li></ul>

| Increase sales of potato chips to teens. | • Distribute free samples or discount coupons at high school football games.
• Sponsor an event attended by teens. |

In your Action Programs section, you will describe the steps that need to be taken in detail, when they should be done, who will do them, and so on.

5. Strategy and Implementation (Sales and Distribution)

In the Strategy and Implementation section, describe how your products and customers "meet" or come together through sales and distribution.

Describe your sales philosophies and methods. Do you employ an aggressive sales method for a large number of quick sales, or a relaxed method where the emphasis is on having customers feel comfortable to come back another time even if they do not buy now? Do you use contract sales people or employees? Explain your approach to sales issues.

a.   Strategy

Describe your distribution system. (Where will your product be placed so customers have access to it?) A few points about distribution to address in your marketing plan are:

- Is the exchange of the product made in a store? Through the mail? Through a direct sales representative?

- What are your production and inventory capacities? (How quickly can you make products and how many can you store?)

- Are there cyclical fluctuations or seasonal demands for your products? For example, if you produce Christmas decorations, how will you manage peak production and sales periods as well as slow periods?

- Do you sell to individuals or to re-sellers? Your company may use more than one method. For example, you may sell directly to customers who place large orders, but also sell to customers who buy small quantities of your product through retail outlets.

b.   Implementation: Action Programs

In the Action Programs section of your marketing plan, you are basically developing a very detailed promotions "to do" list. It is a task list that describes what will be done, when it will begin or be completed, who will accomplish the tasks, and so on.

The Action Program picks up where the promotion plan leaves off. Whereas the Promotion Plan might state that your company will participate in industry trade shows, the Action Program lists the trade shows and their dates, your objectives for attending each one, which company representatives will be sent, the results you expect, the marketing tactics you will employ, and so on.

Action programs can be formatted in a chart, table, and timeline or in any other way. Programs can be grouped chronologically or by event types. For example, you could list all the activities planned in each month, or you could group similar activities, such as public relations activities, together regardless of when they'll occur during the year.

If your action plan becomes too lengthy, you might decide that it is better to place some of the more detailed bits of information—such as a media placement plan outlining where and when ads will run for an advertising campaign—in the supporting documents section.

How Much Will It Cost?

Your Marketing Budget

Estimate the cost of the marketing activities you have described in the marketing plan so
you will have a budget to keep everyone on track over the course of the year. Typical marketing expense categories are marketing communications, market research, promotions, advertising, events, and public relations.

Because marketing needs and costs vary widely, there are no simple rules for determining what your marketing budget should be. As mentioned earlier, a popular method with small business owners is to allocate a small percentage of gross sales from the most recent year. This usually amounts to about 2 percent for an existing business. However, if you are planning on launching a new product or business, you may want to increase your marketing budget figure to as much as 10 percent of your expected gross sales. Another method used by small business owners is to analyze and estimate the competition's budget and either match or exceed it.

Conclusion

Would you ever head out on a cross-country trip without a map or GPS? I didn't think so, unless you want to get lost and waste a lot of valuable time. Starting a marketing effort without a plan is no different.

Knowing what marketing efforts you will focus on, what your competition is doing, and what your strengths and weaknesses are, will point you in the proper direction. Writing out your company mission statement and marketing plan will not only guide your marketing and advertisement efforts for financial success, but will also ensure that you can get there from here.

Resources

- **Marketing Plan Pro**
  www.paloalto.com
  Marketing Plan Pro includes everything you need to create a professional, complete, and accurate marketing plan. Whether you are presenting a marketing plan to your department, working for a Fortune 500 company or simply looking for a marketing direction for your small business, Marketing Plan Pro software has all the tools and features you need.

- **SBA**
  www.sba.gov
  Careful planning is fundamental to success. The SBA Small Business Planner includes information and resources that will help you at any stage of the business lifecycle. Here you will find numerous guides to help you develop your marketing program. If marketing to the U.S. government is in your future, you will find helpful tips and links to assist you.

[Strategy 10]

The High-Performance Entrepreneur Develops a Business Plan

David P. Hale, PhD

When I started out in business, I spent a great deal of time researching every detail that might be pertinent to the deal I was interested in making. I still do the same today. People often comment on how quickly I operate, but the reason I can move quickly is that I've done the background work first, which no one usually sees. I prepare myself thoroughly, and then when it is time to move ahead, I am ready to sprint.

Donald Trump

A business plan should be a work-in-progress, a living, breathing document that is updated on a regular basis. Even successful, growing businesses should maintain a current business plan. Think of your business plan as your GPS to success and the tool to direct you along your business path.

As any good salesperson realizes, you have to know everything you can about your products or services in order to persuade someone to buy them. In this discussion, you are the salesperson and your products represent your business. Your customers are potential investors and employees. Since you want your customers to believe in you, you must be able to convince them that you know what you are talking about when it comes to your business.

To become an expert (or to fine-tune your knowledge if you already believe you are one), you must be willing to roll up your sleeves and begin digging through information. Since not all information that you gather will be relevant to the development of your business plan, it will help you to know what you are looking for before you get started. In order to help you with this process, an outline of the essential elements of a good business plan is included. Remember, your business plan is your roadmap or GPS to business success.

Why the High-Performance Entrepreneur Needs a Business Plan

A business plan precisely defines your business, identifies your goals, and serves as your company's resume. Its basic components include a current and pro forma balance sheet, an income statement, and a cash flow analysis. It helps you allocate resources properly, handle unforeseen complications, and make the right decisions. As it provides specific and organized information about your company and how you will repay borrowed money, a good business plan is a crucial part of any loan package. Additionally, it can tell your sales personnel, suppliers, and others about your operations and goals.

Why You Need to Define Your Business in Detail

It may seem silly to ask yourself, "What business am I really in?" but some owner/managers have gone broke because they never answered that question. One watch store owner realized that most of his time was spent repairing watches, while most of his money was spent selling them. He finally decided he was in the repair business and discontinued the sales operations. His profits improved dramatically.

Using Your Business Plan

A business plan is a tool with three basic purposes: *communication, management,* and *planning.* As a *communication tool,* it is used to attract investment capital, secure loans, convince people to work for you, and assist in attracting strategic business partners. The development of a comprehensive business plan shows whether a business has the potential to make a profit. It requires a realistic look at almost every phase of business and allows you to show that you have worked out all the problems and decided on potential alternatives before actually launching your business.

As a *management tool,* the business plan helps you track, monitor, and evaluate your progress. The business plan is a living document that you will modify as you gain knowledge and experience. By using your business plan to establish timelines and benchmarks, you can gauge your progress and compare your projections to actual accomplishments.

As a *planning tool*, the business plan guides you through the various phases of your business. A thoughtful plan will help identify roadblocks and obstacles so that you can avoid them and establish alternatives. Many business owners share their business plans with their employees to foster a broader understanding of where the business is going.

Finding Your Market Niche

A market in its entirety is too broad in scope for any but the largest companies to tackle successfully. The best strategy for a smaller business is to divide demand into manageable market niches. Small operations can then offer specialized goods and services attractive to a specific group of prospective buyers.

There are undoubtedly specific products or services you are especially suited to provide within your field. Study the market carefully and you will find opportunities. As an example, surgical instruments used to be sold in bulk to both small medical practices and large hospitals. One firm realized that smaller medical offices could not afford to sterilize instruments after each use like hospitals did, but instead simply disposed of them. The firm's sales representatives talked to surgeons and hospital workers to learn what would be more suitable for them.

Based on this information, the company developed disposable instruments, which could be sold in larger quantities at a lower cost. Another firm capitalized on the fact that hospital operating rooms must carefully count the instruments used before and after surgery. This firm met that particular need by packaging their instruments in pre-counted, customized sets for different forms of surgery.

While researching your own company's niche, consider the results of your market survey and the areas in which your competitors are already firmly situated. Put this information into a table or a graph to illustrate where an opening might exist for your product or service. Try to find the right configuration of products, services, quality, and price that will ensure the least direct competition. Unfortunately, there is no universally effective way to make these comparisons. For example, only someone who had already thought of developing pre-packaged surgical instruments could use a survey to determine whether a market actually existed for them. This means looking at what the competition is doing and then figuring out how you can do it better.

A well-designed database can help you sort through your market information and reveal particular segments you might not see otherwise. For example, do customers in a certain geographic area tend to purchase products that combine high quality and high price more frequently? Do your small business clients take advantage of your customer service more often than larger ones? If so, consider focusing on being a local provider of high quality goods and services or a service-oriented company that pays extra attention to small businesses.

If you do target a new niche market, make sure that this niche does not conflict with your overall business plan. For example, a small bakery that makes cookies by hand cannot go after a market for inexpensive, mass-produced cookies, regardless of the demand.

Plan Your Work

The importance of a comprehensive, thoughtful business plan cannot be over-emphasized. Many things hinge on the business plan, such as outside funding, credit from suppliers, management of your operation and finances, promotion and marketing of your business, and achievement of your goals and objectives.

Despite the critical importance of a business plan, many entrepreneurs drag their feet when it comes to preparing a written document. They argue that their marketplace changes too fast for a business plan to be useful or that they just do not have enough time, but just as a builder will not begin construction without a blueprint, eager business owners should not rush into new ventures without a plan. In this case, your business plan will provide a written foundation from which to build a successful company.

Before you begin writing your business plan, consider four critical core questions:
What service or product does your business provide and what needs does it fill?

_____

_____

_____

_____

Who are the potential customers for your product or service and why will they purchase it from you rather than your competitors?

_____

_____

_____

_____

How will you reach your potential customers?

_____

_____

_____

_____

Where will you get the financial resources to start your business?

_____

_____

_____

_____

Writing Your Business Plan

Every successful business plan should include something about each of the following areas, since these are what make up the essentials of a good business plan:

- Executive Summary
- Company Organization and Management
- Market Analysis
- Service and Product Line
- Sales and Promotion
- Financials
- Appendix

Part 1: The Executive Summary (Cover Letter)

The Executive Summary is the most important section of your business plan. It provides a concise overview of the entire plan along with a history of your company. This section tells your reader where your company is and where you want to take it. It is the first thing your readers see; therefore, it is the piece that will either grab their interest and make them want to keep reading or make them want to put it down and forget about it. More than anything else, this section is important because it tells the reader why you think your business idea will be successful.

The Executive Summary should be the last section you write. After you have worked out all the details of your plan, you will be in a better position to summarize it—and it should be a summary (i.e., no more than four pages, and preferably one or two). Think of the Executive Summary as your mini business plan.

Contents of the Executive Summary

- The Mission Statement: The mission statement briefly explains the thrust of your business. It could be two words, two sentences, a paragraph, or even a single image. It should be as direct and focused as possible, and it should leave the reader with a clear mental picture of what your business purpose is.

- Birth date of your business.

- Names of founders, functions they perform, and their experience.

- Products manufactured/services rendered.

- Location of business, branches, or subsidiaries and markets.

- How much money are you requesting and how will it be paid off?

- Who is your prime competition?

- Summary of company growth including financial or market highlights (e.g., your company doubled its worth in a twelve-month period; you became the first company in your industry to provide a certain service).

- Summary of management's plans: With the exception of the mission statement, all of the information in the Executive Summary should be highlighted in a brief, even bulleted, fashion. Remember, these facts are laid out in-depth further along in the plan.

If you are just starting a business, you will not have a lot of information to plug into the areas mentioned above. Instead, focus on your experience and background as well as the decisions that led you to start this particular enterprise. Include information about the problems your target market has and what solutions you provide. Show how the expertise you have will allow you to make significant inroads into the market. Tell your reader what you are going to do differently or better. Convince the reader that there is a need for your service or product, then go ahead and address your (the company's) plans.

To assist the reader in locating specific sections in your business plan, include a table of contents directly following the executive summary. Make sure that the content titles are very broad; in other words, avoid detailed descriptions in your table of contents.

Funding Request

In this section, you will request the amount of funding you will need to start or expand your business. If necessary, you can include different funding scenarios, such as a best and worst-case scenario, but remember that later, in the financial section, you must be able to back up these requests and scenarios with corresponding financial statements.

You will want to include the following in this section: your current funding requirement, your future funding requirements over the next five years, how you will use the funds you receive, and any long-range financial strategies you are planning that would have any type of impact on your funding request.

When you are outlining your current and future funding requirements, be sure to include the amount you want now and the amount you want in the future, the time period that each request will cover, the type of funding you would like to have (i.e., equity, debt), and the terms that you would like to have applied.

How you will use your funds is very important to a creditor. Is the funding request for capital expenditures? Working capital? Debt retirement? Acquisitions? Whatever it is, be sure to list it in this section.

Last of all, make sure that you include any strategic information related to your business that may have an impact on your financial situation in the future, such as: going public with your company, having a leveraged buyout, being acquired by another company, the method with which you will service your debt, or whether or not you plan to sell your business in the future. Each of these is extremely important to a future creditor, since they will directly impact your ability to repay your loan(s).

January 5, 2008

Tomorrow's Biz Bank
1234 Main Street
Tomorrow, CA 12345

Re: Loan Request for $200,000

Dear Ms. Johnson,

With 24 years of managerial and corporate training experience, we are requesting a loan to start a training and development consultancy, named Tomorrow's Biz.

The environment for a managerial training and development company in today's corporate culture is ripe for growth. During 2006, corporations spent over five billion dollars on training and development seminars. This represents a 15 percent increase over the previous year.

Our niche market is the small business environment. I plan to reach potential clients with target marketing, which you will read about in the business plan. Additionally, we have working relationships with several training organizations and have proposed on-going cooperative training contracts with each.

One of our three local competitors is a technical college, which has five branches throughout the city. The other two are university-led, small-business development centers, though they are deficient in niche expertise.

We are investing $50,000 in personal savings and requesting a loan of $200,000 from your bank. We wish to repay this over ten years, using the cash flow from the business. As a secondary source of repayment, we will use our homes and additional personal assets, valued at $200,000 as collateral.

Our business plan is attached. In it you will find the information you will need. Any questions you may have may be directed to the undersigned at (123) 456-7890.

Thank you for your time,

David P. Hale

Template:

Date: _____

Lender Name & Address: _____
_____
_____
_____

Re: Loan Request for $_____

Dear _____ (lender's name)

I am requesting a loan in the amount of _____. As the owner, I have _____ years of experience in the _____ industry including _____ (include experience or training that qualifies you to run this business).

The market for this business (include a brief paragraph about the industry and its growth potential)
_____
_____
_____
_____

My market area is (include a brief paragraph about your target market area and customers)
_____
_____
_____

My competition in this market includes (include a brief paragraph about your competitors and how you will draw their business) _____
_____
_____
_____

I am investing $ _____ of my own funds. I will use personal assets valued at $ _____ and business assets valued at $ _____ as collateral.

Attached is a copy of our business plan that backs up our request. If you have any questions, please contact _____ (your name) at _____ (phone number).

Thank you very much for your time and consideration,

_____   _____
Signature   Printed Name

Part 2: Company Organization and Management

Without going into detail, this section should include a high-level look at how all of the different elements of your business fit together. The company description section should include information about the nature of your business and list the primary factors that you believe will make your business successful.

When defining the nature of your business (or why you're in business), be sure to list the marketplace needs that you are trying to satisfy. Include the ways in which you plan to satisfy these needs using your products or services. Finally, list the specific individuals and/or organizations that you have identified as having these needs.

Primary success factors might include a superior ability to satisfy your customers' needs, highly efficient methods of delivering your product or service, outstanding personnel, or a key location. Each of these would give your business a competitive advantage.

This section should include your company's organizational structure, details about the ownership of your company, profiles of your management team, and the qualifications of your board of directors.

Who does what in your business? What is their background and why are you bringing them into the business as board members or employees? What are their responsibilities? These may seem like unnecessary questions to answer in a one- or two-person organization, but the people reading your business plan want to know who is in charge, so tell them. Give a detailed description of each division or department and its function.

What kind of salary and benefits package do you have for your people? What incentives are you offering? Assure your reader that the people you have on staff are more than just names on a letterhead.

Organizational Structure

A simple but effective way to lay out the structure of your company is to create an organizational chart with a narrative description. This will prove that you are leaving nothing to chance, you have thought out exactly who is doing what, and there is someone in charge of every function of your company. Nothing will fall through the cracks, and nothing will be done three or four times over. To a potential investor or employee, that is very important.

Ownership Information

This section should also include the legal structure of your business along with the subsequent ownership information it relates to. Have you incorporated your business? If so, is it a C or S corporation? On the other hand, perhaps you have formed a partnership with someone. If so, is it a general or limited partnership? Or, maybe you are a sole proprietor.

Important ownership information that should be incorporated into your business plan includes:

- Names of owners
- Percentage ownership
- Extent of involvement with the company
- Forms of ownership (i.e., common stock, preferred stock, general partner, limited partner)
- Outstanding equity equivalents (i.e., options, warrants, convertible debt)
- Common stock (i.e., authorized or issued)

Management Profiles

Experts agree that one of the strongest factors for success in any growth company is the ability and record of accomplishment of its owner/management, so let your reader know about the key people in your company and their backgrounds. Provide resumes that include the following information:

- Name
- Position (include brief position description along with primary duties)
- Primary responsibilities and authority
- Education
- Unique experience and skills
- Prior employment
- Special skills
- Past track record
- Industry recognition
- Community involvement
- Number of years with company

- Compensation basis and levels (make sure these are reasonable—not too high or too low)

Be sure you quantify achievements (e.g., "Managed a sales force of ten people," "Managed a department of fifteen people," "Increased revenue by 15 percent in the first six months," "Expanded the retail outlets at the rate of two each year," "Improved the customer service as rated by our customers from a 60 percent to a 90 percent rating"). Much like a personal resume, your business plan should provide visualization through numbers.

Also, highlight how the people surrounding you complement your own skills. If you are just starting out, show how each person's unique experience will contribute to the success of your venture.

Board of Director's Qualifications

The major benefit of an unpaid advisory board is that it can provide expertise that your company cannot otherwise afford. A list of well-known, successful business owners/managers can go a long way toward enhancing your company's credibility and perception of management expertise.

If you have a board of directors, be sure to gather the following information when developing the outline for your business plan:

- Names
- Positions on the board
- Extent of involvement with company
- Background
- Historical and future contribution to the company's success

Management Summary

The initial management team depends on the founders themselves, with little backup. As it grows, Tomorrow's Biz will establish a team that includes five employees who operate under a president and an office manager.

The management philosophy is based on responsibility and mutual respect. People who work at Tomorrow's Biz want to work at the company because it has an environment that encourages "E³T," which is: Energized Excellence Every Time. This E³T concept is our tool in performing the client's value creation of Tomorrow's Biz.

Personnel Plan

The team includes five employees, under a president and an office manager.

The three main management divisions are Sales and Marketing, Operations, and Internal Business Management. The departments managed by the Sales and Marketing division are: marketing, sales, products and services, research and development, and public relations operations. The departments managed by the Internal Business Management division are: operations, human resources, accounting, and information management.

Part 3: Market Analysis and Strategy Implementation

The market analysis section should illustrate your knowledge about your particular business industry. It should also present general highlights and conclusions of any marketing research data you have collected; however, the specific details of your marketing research studies should be moved to the Appendix section of your business plan.

This section should include an industry description and outlook, target market information, market test results, lead times, and an evaluation of your competition.

Industry Description and Outlook

This overview section should include a description of your primary industry, the current size of the industry as well as its historic growth rate, trends and characteristics related to the industry as a whole (i.e., What life cycle stage is the industry in? What is its projected growth rate?), and the major customer groups within the industry (i.e., businesses, governments, consumers, etc.).

Identifying Your Target Market

Your target market is simply the market (or group of customers) that you want to target (or focus on and sell to). When you are defining your target market, it is important to narrow it to a manageable size; many businesses make the mistake of trying to be everything to everybody. Often times, this philosophy leads to failure.

In this section, you should gather information that identifies:

- Distinguishing characteristics of the major/primary market you are targeting. This section might include information about the critical needs of your potential customers, the degree to which those needs are (or are not) currently being met, and the demographics of the group. It would also include the geographic location of your target market, the identification of the major decision makers, and any seasonal or cyclical trends that may affect the industry or your business.

- Size of the primary target market. Here, you would need to know the number of potential customers in your primary market, the number of annual purchases they make in products or services similar to your own, the geographic area they reside in, and the forecasted market growth for this group.

- The extent to which you feel you will be able to gain market share and the reasons why. In this research, you would determine the market share percentage and number of customers you expect to obtain in a defined geographic area. You would also outline the logic you used to develop these estimates.

- Your pricing and gross margin targets. Here, you would define the levels of your pricing, your gross margin levels, and any discount structures that you plan to set up for your business, such as volume/bulk discounts or prompt payment discounts.

- Resources for finding information related to your target market. These resources might include directories, trade association publications, and government documents.

- Media you will use to reach your target audience. These might include publications, radio or television broadcasts, or any other type of credible source that may have influence with your target market.

- Purchasing cycle of your potential customers. Here, you will need to identify the needs of your target market, do research to find the solutions to their needs, evaluate the solutions you come up with, and finally, identify who actually has the authority to choose the final solution.

- Trends and potential changes that may impact your primary target market. Key characteristics of your secondary markets. Just like with your primary target market, here you would again want to identify the needs, demographics, and the significant trends that will influence your secondary markets in the future.

Market Tests

When you are including information about any of the market tests you have completed for your business plan, be sure to focus only on the results of these tests. Any specific details should be included in the Appendix. Market test results might include the potential customers who were contacted, any information or demonstrations that were given to prospective customers, how important it is to satisfy the target market's needs, and the target market's desire to purchase your business's products or services at varying prices.

Lead-Times

Lead-time is the amount of time between when a customer places an order and when the product or service is actually delivered. When you are researching this information, determine what your lead-time will be for the initial order, reorders, and volume purchases.

Competitive Analysis

When you are doing a competitive analysis, you need to identify your competition by product line or service as well as by market segment; assess their strengths and weaknesses, determine how important your target market is to your competitors, and identify any barriers that may hinder you as you are entering the market.

Be sure to identify all of your key competitors for each of your products or services. For each key competitor, determine what their market share is, then try to estimate how long it will take before new competitors will enter into the marketplace.

In other words, what is your window of opportunity? Finally, identify any indirect or secondary competitors that may have an impact on your business's success.

The strengths of your competitors are also competitive advantages, which you too can provide. The strengths of your competitors may take many forms, but the most common include:

- An ability to satisfy customer needs
- A large share of the market and the consumer awareness that comes with it
- A good track record and reputation
- Solid financial resources and the subsequent staying power which that provides
- Key personnel

Weaknesses are simply the opposite of strengths. In other words, analyze the same areas as you did before to determine what your competitors' weaknesses are. Are they unable to satisfy their customers' needs? Do they have poor market penetration? Is their record of accomplishment or reputation not up to par? Do they have limited financial resources? Can they not retain good people? All of these can be red flags for any business. If you find weak areas in your competition, be sure to find out why they are having problems. This way, you can avoid the same mistakes they have made.

If your target market is not important to your competition, then you will most likely have an open field to run in if your idea is a good one—at least for a while. However, if the competition is keen for your target market, be prepared to overcome some barriers. Barriers to any market might include:

- A high investment cost
- The time it takes to set up your business
- Changing technology
- The lack of quality personnel
- Customer resistance (i.e., long-standing relationships, brand loyalty)
- Existing patents and trademarks that you cannot infringe upon

Regulatory Restrictions

The final area that you should look at as you are researching this section is regulatory restrictions. This includes information related to current customer or governmental regulatory requirements as well as any changes that may be upcoming. Specific details that you need to find out include the methods for meeting any of the requirements that will affect your business, the timing involved (i.e., How long do you have to comply? When do the requirements go into effect?), and the costs involved.

Market Analysis Summary

Tomorrow's Biz has a unique offering of services that appeal to a large customer base. The company will concentrate on small businesses because they provide the maximum profit potential. The following sections outline key information regarding the target market.

Market Segmentation

The groups of potential customers for Tomorrow's Biz are listed in the order of preference:

- Small Business (less than 100 employees)
- Medium Companies
- Large Corporations
- Government Agencies
- Individual Clients

***You can add a chart here depicting the number of companies in each category within your market.

Target Market Segment Strategy

As indicated by the previous chart and table, Tomorrow's Biz must focus on the small business and Web-based market along with individual customers, who will be the core customer base.

Service Business Analysis

The following companies are major players in the small business development and coaching business:

- Small Business Administration
- Small Business Development Centers
- Main Street University
- South End Community College

Competition and Buying Patterns

Recent analysis has indicated that training, development, and coaching costs in the United States have risen by 15 percent in the previous three years. This analysis is based upon a 20 percent rise in small business startups and expansion. This can be related to the soaring e-business development evolution. To take advantage of this situation, Tomorrow's Biz will utilize Web-based training along with live and distance-learning options.

Strategy and Implementation Summary

Tomorrow's Biz will focus on the following three technological market segments:

- Small and home businesses. This is the most important market segment. These companies will be interacting with Tomorrow's Biz for training and development programs that are more effective when spun off than when managed in-house.

- Medium-sized organizations. For high-growth fields, such as software and multimedia, Tomorrow's Biz will offer an attractive development alternative that will allow the company to deliver training via Web-based modules.

- Individual clients. Upper echelon people such as C-level executives, board of directors, managers, and high potential employees. On several occasions, Tomorrow's Biz has teamed up with its end-users in a consortium partnership to perform projects.

Tomorrow's Biz combines unparalleled quality with a cost-effective package to create a coaching service with many competitive advantages. The seasoned management is qualified for several services, such as: small-business development, interpersonal communication improvement, Web presence packages, and the development of Web identity.

We provide this range of services to anyone from high-level management firms to home businesses; clients can always count on quick, accurate services from the company.

Part 4: Services and Product Line

What are you selling? In this section, describe your service or product, emphasizing the benefits to potential and current customers. For example, do not tell your readers which exercises you will make them perform as a personal trainer. Tell them why busy gym-goers will prefer your services and routines, which are based on their personal goals and body type. Your overall program delivers quick results with a minimum of workouts.

Focus on the areas where you have a distinct advantage. Identify the problem in your target market for which your service or product provides a solution. Give the reader hard evidence that people are, or will be, willing to pay for your solution. List your company's services and products and attach any marketing/promotional materials. Provide details regarding suppliers, availability of products/services, and service or product costs. Also, include information addressing new services or products that will soon be added to the company's line.

Overall, this section should include:

- Detailed description of your product or service (from your customers' perspective). Here, you would need to include information about the specific benefits of your product or service. You would also want to talk about your product/service's ability to meet consumer needs, any advantages your product has over that of the competition, and the present development stage your product is in (i.e., idea, prototype, etc.).

- Information related to your product's life cycle. Be sure to include information about where your product or service is in its life cycle, as well as any factors that may influence its cycle in the future.

- Any copyright, patent, and trade secret information that may be relevant. Here, you need to include information related to existing, pending, or anticipated copyright and patent filings along with any key characteristics of your products/services that you cannot obtain a copyright or patent for. You should also incorporate key aspects of your products and services that may be classified as trade secrets. Last, but not least, be sure to add any information pertaining to existing legal agreements, such as nondisclosure or non-compete agreements.

- Research and development activities you are involved in or are planning to explore. R&D activities would include any in-process or future activities related to the development of new products/services. This section would also include information about what you expect the results of future R&D activities to be. Be sure to analyze the R&D efforts of not only your own business, but also that of others in your industry.

SERVICES

Tomorrow's Biz is a Web-based training and development consulting firm specializing in the marketing of a comprehensive set of integrated professional services that provide our customers with high-quality consulting services for small business development, training seminars on interpersonal communication, job search strategies, Web presence, branding, and coaching services on a global scale.

Service Description

Tomorrow's Biz offers expertise in the coaching, training, and development services it delivers. With an abundance of experience in these fields, the firm is able to sell and package its services in various platforms that allow clients to choose their preferred benefits. These may include:

- Retainer coaching
- Project consulting
- In-house training
- Web-based training

Competitive Comparison

Within its niche, Tomorrow's Biz does not have any competitors, but rather "prospective business partners." This is because our company provides our clients with solutions as well as value creations. Its services have been sought out by companies ranging from high-level management firms to international training and development corporations. Companies choosing to do small-business development, managerial and communication training, along with building branding and Web presence will select Tomorrow's Biz to deliver the following value creations:

- Improved interpersonal communication
- Web identity
- Branding of services
- New ways of adding value

Sales Literature

The business began with a general business pamphlet, brochure, and video calling card. These items were included in last year's startup expenses. Sales literature for the market will remain important.

Fulfillment

The key fulfillment and delivery of services will be by live and Web-based training and coaching. The core value is professional expertise provided through a combination of experience, intelligent work, discipline, on-going improvements, and education.

Technology

Tomorrow's Biz maintains the latest Windows capabilities including:

- Internet capabilities for working with clients directly through e-mail delivery of reports and information.
- Ability to prepare and deliver multimedia presentations in formats including, disk, live, or video.
- Desktop publishing for delivery of regular reports, projects, and marketing reports and materials.

Part 5: Sales Strategies and Promotion

Marketing is the process of creating customers, and customers are the lifeblood of your business. In this section, the first thing you want to do is define your marketing strategy. There is no single way to approach a marketing strategy; your strategy should be part of an ongoing self-evaluation process and unique to your company. However, there are steps you can follow that will help you think through the strategy you would like to use.

Your Overall Marketing Strategy Should Include:

- Market penetration strategy.
- Strategy for growing your business. This growth strategy might include: an internal strategy such as how to increase your human resources, an acquisition strategy such as buying another business, a franchise strategy for branching out, a horizontal strategy where you would provide the same type of products to different users, or a vertical strategy where you would continue providing the same products but would offer them at different levels of the distribution chain.

- Channels of distribution strategy. Choices for distribution channels could include: original equipment manufacturers (OEMs), an internal sales force, distributors, or retailers.

- Communication strategy. How are you going to reach your customers? Usually some combination of the following works the best: promotions, advertising, public relations, personal selling, and printed materials such as brochures, catalogs, flyers, etc.

Once you have defined your marketing strategy, you can then define your sales strategy. How do you plan to sell your product?

Your Overall Sales Strategy Should Include:

- A sales force strategy. If you are going to have a sales force, do you plan to use internal or independent representatives? How many salespeople will you recruit for your sales force? What type of recruitment strategies will you use? How will you train your sales force? What about compensation for your sales force?

- Your sales activities. When you are defining your sales strategy, it is important that you break it down into activities. For instance, you need to identify your prospects. Once you have made a list of your prospects, you need to prioritize it. Next, identify the number of sales calls you will make over a certain time frame. From there, you need to determine the average number of sales calls you will need to make per sale, the average dollar size per sale, and the average dollar size per vendor.

Sales Strategy

Tomorrow's Biz's strategy focuses first on maintaining the identity of the high-end buyer who appreciates quality service, but is also very demanding regarding value creations. Tomorrow's Biz has been able to find these customers using a combination of social and interactive e-mail relationships.

Furthermore, as a part of its "individual sales strategy," to ensure optimum client satisfaction, Tomorrow's Biz customizes its services for each specific client. This approach is called "individual performance strategy" because customization permits clients to participate in producing exactly what they want.

Even when a business offers a standard service, it is not making a standard sales offer. The customer is able to choose a tailored offering mix of elements, such as optional services benefits, delivery conditions, training, financing alternatives, technical services options, sales assistance options, etc.

Sales Forecast

The sales forecast monthly summary is included in the Appendix. The annual sales projections are included here in the following chart and table.

The sales forecast assumes that the yearly change in costs or prices will average 20 percent, which is a reasonable assumption based on the last few years.

Tomorrow's Biz is expecting to increase sales modestly in 2008 and 2009, with sales growth accelerating in 2010 through 2012. It is the expectation that the company will double its starting sales within five years.
*** You may insert forecasting spreadsheet and graphs here.

Milestones

The accompanying chart and table show specific milestones with responsibilities assigned, dates, and budgets. Tomorrow's Biz is focusing on a few key milestones that are to be accomplished. Print advertising will target newspapers and magazines, while Internet advertising will appear on both Web sites and search engines.

***You may insert a timeline spreadsheet here if desired.

Part 6: Financials

The financials should be developed after you have analyzed your market and set clear goals. That is when you can allocate resources efficiently. The following items are the critical financial statements to include in your business plan.

Historical Financial Data

If you own an established business, you will be requested to supply historical data related to your company's performance. Most creditors request data for the last three to five years, depending on the length of time you have been in business.

The historical financial data to include would be your company's income statements, balance sheets, and cash flow statements for each year you have been in business (usually for up to three to five years). Often creditors are also interested in any collateral you may have that could be used to ensure your loan, regardless of the stage of your business.

Prospective Financial Data

All businesses, whether startup or growing, will be required to supply prospective financial data. Most of the time, creditors will want to see what you expect your company to be able to do within the next five years. Each year's documents should include forecasted income statements, balance sheets, cash flow statements, and capital expenditure budgets. For the first year, you should supply monthly or quarterly projections. After that, you can stretch it to quarterly and/or yearly projections for years two through five.

Make sure that your projections match your funding requests; creditors will be on the lookout for inconsistencies. It is much better if you catch mistakes before they do. If you have made assumptions in your projections, be sure to summarize what you have assumed. This way, the reader will not be left guessing.

Finally, include a short analysis of your financial information. Include a ratio and trend analysis for all of your financial statements (both historical and prospective). Since pictures speak louder than words, you may want to add graphs of your trend analysis (especially if they are positive).

Hints for Developing Your Financials

- Make realistic assumptions. Lenders know there are risks, so explain how they will be handled. They like to see business owners who recognize and solve them. Make a record of your assumptions so you can prove to the lender that your projections are realistic.

- Show reasonable links between the past (if buying a business), actual, and future projections.

Watch for These Common Financial Problems

- Limited finances. Finances is just another word for money, and if there is not enough of it, it can lead to insufficient working capital (money for day-to-day operations). Do not try to make money stretch too far. Ask for more money, or cut down on liabilities and expenses.

- Little or no record keeping. You must keep meticulous records for yourself, the IRS, and your lender.

- Failure to seek outside help. Consult an accountant, gain business advisors, contact the SBA (www.sba.gov) or your state's Department of Economic Development. Your advisors' input is valuable, but do not be totally dependent on them. Educate yourself. You should have a basic understanding of your company's finances. Know how to read your own financial statements and reports.

- Poor management. A business needs a good financial manager (within or outside the company). It is your money, so be very self-disciplined.

- Reluctance to invest in the business. Why should the lender stand behind you if you will not invest any of your own money? You must put a percentage of your own money into the company (usually 25 percent to 50 percent).

- Failure to personally guarantee the loan repayment. If the business fails for any reason, the owners must repay the loan. Lenders need to be assured of your total commitment.

Personal Financial Statement

Complete a personal financial statement for each person listed in the business plan who will be guaranteeing the loan. It is a good idea to order your credit reports from the three credit bureaus previously mentioned in this manual and review it because lenders will look it over with a fine-tooth comb. Be prepared to explain any negative reports.

Part 7: The Appendix

The Appendix section should be provided to readers on an as-needed basis. In other words, it should not be included with the main body of your business plan. Your plan is your communication tool; as such, it will be seen by many people. Some of the information in the business section you will not want everyone to see, but specific individuals (such as creditors) may want access to this information in order to make lending decisions. Therefore, it is important to have the Appendix within easy reach.

The Appendix should include:

- Credit history (personal and business)
- Resumes of key managers
- Product pictures
- Letters of reference
- Details of market studies
- Relevant magazine articles or book references
- Licenses, permits, or patents
- Legal documents
- Copies of leases
- Building permits
- Contracts
- List of business consultants, including attorney and accountant

Any copies of your business plan should be controlled; keep a distribution record. This will allow you to update and maintain your business plan on an as-needed basis. Remember, too, that you should include a private placement disclaimer with your business plan if you plan to use it to raise capital.

Conclusion

As with your marketing, the High-Performance Entrepreneur also writes out a clear, concise, and focused business plan. As explained earlier in the book, if you are planning on seeking a loan, you will definitely need to write a business plan.

A proper business plan gives you the guidance you need to propel your business in the right direction. It also shows potential lenders that you are planning to be successful. The number one reason entrepreneurs fail at a business venture is a lack of planning.

Many an entrepreneur has attempted to develop their grassroots venture without writing a business plan. Granted, a few will succeed, but at what cost? More than likely, they will confront setback after setback and waste valuable time and resources. If they are not succeeding, without a written business plan it will be difficult for them to understand why they are failing.

If you truly desire to be a High-Performance Entrepreneur, take the time to properly write a business plan. If you find it difficult, check out the resources below for examples and guidance.

Resources

• **Canadian Business Resource Center in British Columbia**
www.cbsc.org/ibp/en/index.cfm
A step-by-step business planning tool for new or existing businesses.

• **Business Plan Pro**
www.paloalto.com
The top business-plan writing software on the market by Palo Alto Software.

[Strategy 11]

The High-Performance Entrepreneur Pays Taxes and Insurance

David P. Hale, PhD

But in this world nothing is certain but death and taxes.
Benjamin Franklin

Taxes

Tax laws change on an annual basis, so it is important to make sure you and your company are up-to-date on the latest changes. You can accomplish this by visiting the IRS Web site (www.irs.gov and www.irs.gov/smallbiz). The IRS has numerous free resources to help you navigate the business tax requirements.

Because of the intricacies of your own business situation, I will highlight some of the more important areas of taxation and insurance of which to pay attention. You will serve yourself and your business wisely by seeking the services of a competent tax attorney, accountant, and insurance provider about your particular business and what taxes you are required to pay.

It is just as important to notify your state and local taxation offices that you are in business. You can find your state tax offices through your state government Web site or by going to www.taxsites.com/states.html. The following link to the U. S. Chamber of Commerce provides information for each state and points of contact: www.uschamber.com/sb/P07/P07_ 1294.asp.

Business Taxes

The form of business you operate determines what taxes you must pay and how you pay them. The following are the four general types of business taxes.

Income Tax

All businesses except partnerships must file an annual income tax return. If you have a partnership, you will file an information return. The form you use depends on how your business is organized.

The federal income tax is a pay-as-you-go tax. You must pay the tax as you earn or receive income during the year. An employee usually has income tax withheld from his or her pay. If you do not pay your tax through withholding, or do not pay enough tax that way, you might have to pay estimated tax. If you are not required to make estimated tax payments, you may pay any tax due when you file your return. For additional information, refer to Publication 583 (*Starting a Business and Keeping Records*) on the IRS Web site (www.IRS.gov) for more information.

Estimated Tax

Generally, you must pay taxes on income, including self-employment tax, by making regular payments of estimated tax during the year.

Self-Employment Tax

Self-employment tax (SE tax) is a social security and Medicare tax primarily for individuals who work for themselves. Your payments of SE tax contribute to your coverage under the social security system. Social security coverage provides you with retirement, disability, and survivor, along with hospital insurance (Medicare) benefits.

Generally, you must pay SE tax and file Schedule SE (Form 1040) if either of the following applies:

- If your net earnings from self-employment were $400 or more.

- If you work for a church or a qualified church-controlled organization (other than as a minister or member of a religious order) that elected an exemption from social security and Medicare taxes, you are subject to SE tax if you receive $108.28 or more in wages from the church or organization.

Employment Taxes

When you have employees, you as the employer have certain employment tax responsibilities that you must pay and forms you must file. Employment taxes include the following:

- Social security and Medicare taxes

- Federal income tax withholding
- Federal unemployment (FUTA) tax

For additional information, refer to *Employment Taxes for Small Businesses* on the IRS Web site (www.IRS.gov).

Excise Tax

If you are required to pay excise taxes, you will have to file if you do any of the following:

- Manufacture or sell certain products
- Use various kinds of equipment, facilities, or products
- Receive payment for certain services

Form 720—The federal excise taxes reported on Form 720, *Quarterly Federal Excise Tax Return*, consist of several broad categories of taxes, including the following:

- Environmental taxes
- Communications and air transportation taxes
- Fuel taxes
- Tax on the first retail sale of heavy trucks, trailers, and tractors
- Manufacturers taxes on the sale or use of a variety of different articles

Form 2290—There is a federal excise tax on certain trucks, truck tractors, and buses used on public highways. The tax applies to vehicles having a taxable gross weight of 55,000 pounds or more. Report the tax on Form 2290, *Heavy Highway Vehicle Use Tax Return*. For additional information, see the instructions for Form 2290.

State Taxes

Every state levies some form of tax on small businesses, but in some states, some business structures (especially sole proprietorships) have little to no tax imposed. As a sole proprietor, your taxes will fall within your personal income tax.

To learn more about tax structures in any given state, visit the Business Owner's Toolkit site (www.toolkit.cch.com/text/P07_4500.asp) or a list of taxing authorities (www.sba. gov/hotlist/statetaxhomepages.html) in each state.

Insurance

Business insurance is frequently a necessity, not an option. As a business owner, you will have many choices, some far better than others. Becoming an educated business consumer about insurance will pay big dividends.

Buying business insurance is among the best ways to prepare for the unexpected. Without proper protection, misfortunes such as the death of a partner or key employee, embezzlement, a lawsuit, or a natural disaster could spell the end of a thriving operation. Ranging from indispensable worker's compensation insurance to the relatively obscure executive kidnapping coverage, insurance is available for nearly any business risk. Considering the multitude of available options, business owners must carefully weigh whether the cost of certain premiums will justify the coverage for a given risk.

General Liability

Many business owners buy general liability or umbrella liability insurance to cover legal hassles due to claims of negligence. These help protect against payments as the result of bodily injury or property damage, medical expenses, the cost of defending lawsuits, and settlement bonds or judgments required during an appeal procedure.

Product Liability

Every product is capable of personal injury or property damage. Companies that manufacture, wholesale, distribute, and retail a product may be liable for its safety. Additionally, every service rendered may be capable of personal injury or property damage. Businesses are considered liable for negligence, breach of an express or implied warranty, defective products, and defective warnings or instructions.

Home-Based Business Insurance

Contrary to popular belief, homeowner's insurance policies do not generally cover home-based business losses. Commonly needed insurance areas for home-based businesses include business property, professional liability, personal and advertising injury, loss of business data, crime and theft, and disability.

If you operate a home-based business, contact your homeowner's insurance to determine what office items are covered under your policy (i.e. computer, printer, furniture, etc.). You may need to adjust your policy to cover these items.

Internet Business Insurance

Web-based businesses may wish to look into specialized insurance that covers liability for damage done by hackers and viruses. In addition, e-insurance often covers specialized online activities, including lawsuits resulting from Meta tag abuse, banner advertising, or electronic copyright infringement.

Worker's Compensation

Required in every state except Texas, worker's compensation insurance pays for employees' medical expenses and missed wages if injured while working. The amount of insurance employers must carry, rate of payment, and what types of employees must be carried varies depending on the state. In most cases, business owners, independent contractors, domestic employees in private homes, farm workers, and unpaid volunteers are exempt.

Criminal Insurance

No matter how tight security is in your workplace, theft and malicious damage are always possibilities. While the dangers associated with hacking, vandalism, and general theft are obvious, employee embezzlement is more common than most business owners think. Criminal insurance and employee bonds can provide protection against losses in most criminal areas.

Business Interruption Insurance

Some businesses may wish to acquire insurance that covers losses during natural disasters, fires, and other catastrophes that may cause the operation to shut down for a significant amount of time.

Key Person Insurance

In addition to a business continuation plan that outlines how the company will maintain operations if a key person dies, falls ill, or leaves, some companies may wish to buy key person insurance. This type of coverage is usually life insurance that names the corporation as a beneficiary if an essential person dies or is disabled.

Malpractice Insurance

Some licensed professionals need protection against payments as the result of bodily injury or property damage, medical expenses, the cost of defending lawsuits, investigations and settlements, and bonds or judgments required during an appeal procedure.

{Note}: Information in this chapter outlines basic tax and insurance items. Coordinate with your local IRS office and accountant to determine which taxes you are liable for. Additionally, contact a competent insurance agent to discuss the appropriate products for you business situation.

Conclusion

Nothing is worse that the IRS sending you a certified letter stating that you owe back taxes. Sooner or later, they will collect, and the bad part is they want it all at once.

Ensure you check with your local IRS office about what taxes you are required to pay, when you have to pay them, and to whom. Will you, or do you, have employees? Make sure you understand the other taxes you will be required to pay. The resources below will start you off on the right track.

Lastly, next to the IRS knocking on your door, the next worse feeling is being wiped out by a storm or confronted with a lawsuit. Having the proper insurance coverage will provide you with the needed safety net every High-Performance Entrepreneur has.

Resources

- **Chamber of Commerce**
  www.uschamber.com/sb/P07/P07_1294.asp
  Individual state and points of contact.

- **IRS**
  www.irs.gov and www.irs.gov/smallbiz

- **IRS Publication 1066C**, *A Virtual Small Business Tax Workshop* DVD.

- **IRS Publication 583**, *Starting a Business and Keeping Records*
  www.irs.gov/publications/p583/index.html

[Strategy 12]

The High-Performance Entrepreneur Is a Social Networker

Robert T. Uda, MBA

It is estimated that over 80 percent of jobs are found through personal networking rather than help wanted ads. Your use of networking groups will not only broaden your contacts but will also enable you to strengthen your verbal communication skills for those all important job interviews.

Steven Rothberg

What Is Networking?

Networking is defined as establishing contacts, exchanging information, and/or developing relationships with others in informal networks for the purpose of obtaining employment or a job, getting a date, or furthering one's career. The key to networking is to be a good reference and to cultivate good references in informal networks.

Definition of Networking Terms

What is the difference between "reference" and "network"? A "reference" is a *person* who provides either you or someone else (on your behalf) with a letter or phone response (i.e., verification/validation information) of you and your background, capabilities, and desirability. A "reference" is also the *material/information* that a "reference or referrer" gives about you to others. Hence, a "reference" may be both the *person* providing the reference information and the *material/information* itself that is provided.

A "network" is the *list* of names and contact coordinates of your "references." A "network node" is *a specific person* on your network list. Hence, a "network node or networking node" is a specific "reference" or person on your "network" list of references.

Types of Networking

There are several types of networking:

- **Job or Employment Networking**—network to land a new job, business, or customers.
- **Career Networking**—after you land a job, career networking follows to advance your career.
- **Social Networking**—this is a lonely hearts club or networking for dates and/or a future mate.

Focus on Job Networking

If your networking is not helping you get a job or business, helping you meet people who can get you a job or business, or providing you information to help you obtain a job or business, then you are wasting your time networking. Do not mix and confuse career networking with business networking. If you are starting a business and seeking clients, your primary responsibility is to make contacts. Hence, if you are networking, it should be for capturing a contact or a client. After you obtain the business or contact, then you can continue your business-advancement networking.

Networking to create solid business referrals and future contacts is a critical element of your business startup. Keeping in touch with your network contacts must be routinely done on a regular basis … even after you land your most important client.

Referrals really do happen more casually than you might expect. Your college roommate's husband's friend is as likely to land you your next gig as your roommate herself—but only if she knows you're looking for a job when she hears about one.

Networking is extremely important in consulting. I initially started consulting for Hughes Aircraft Company through a good program manager friend of mine. That first gig at Hughes grew into other subsequent consulting gigs, which resulted from networking that I had established while working there.

Barbara Safani, founder of Career Solvers, gives the following seven rules for networking success:

- Ask for information, not a job.
- Be considerate of others' time.
- Listen first; then ask questions.
- Expand your network.
- Follow up.

- Reciprocate.
- Send a thank you letter.

Successful networkers show a sincere interest in their networking contacts. They are constantly developing relations, establishing their credibility, and sharing information. They follow the rules of the game where everyone has something to gain. Like the lottery, you have to be in it to win it.

Social Networking

Author Peter Weddle says, "Networking is one of the best strategies for finding a new or better job. Right? Right. And, social networking clearly involves networking. Right? Right. So, social networking is the new and improved way to land the job or business connection of your dreams. Right? Wrong."

It's hard to miss the buzz about social networking. The media has been all agog over the rapid rise of such sites as MySpace. They attract millions of visitors every month, providing lots of opportunity for individual interaction and relationship building. While this activity is indeed networking, the most important aspect of its description is the adjective that defines it—social. That may be a ton of fun, but it's unlikely to get you hired.

In the past, I've used the term "e-networking" to describe electronic or online networking. However, with the rise of social networking, I've redefined it as "employment networking" or "business networking." E-networking (employment networking) is unlike its very social cousin in three important ways:

- It has a different purpose.
- It is done in a different way.
- It takes place on different Web sites.

Tips on Networking

If you want a new client, start networking now. Marshall Loeb gives these tips on how to get the most out of networking:

- Know what you are looking for.
- Be assertive.
- Curb the desperation and start listening.
- Your most valuable tools include up-to-date company prospectus, business cards, and follow-up phone call or e-mail.
- Stick with it.

Whatever the approach, the bottom line is that we all need to network. By doing so, you will meet people and exchange information that will help you do your job more efficiently. By pursuing any of the many available options, you will build relationships that enrich your life, broaden your horizons, and enhance your business.

Networking with Associates

Networking with your associates is a good thing, especially when you are all looking for jobs or business clients at the same time. As you search for business clients, say on the Internet, you may stumble upon ads that would be a better fit for your other associates. You can then forward those job leads to them.

Now, networking is a two-way street. As you help others, they too will find business leads in their search that may match your background better. If they have received client leads from you, they will feel obligated to return the favor by sending you those client leads that would benefit you. Hence, instead of only you searching for suitable business ads, you may have up to forty-six other associates providing you with suitable leads. How does that increase your productivity? Tremendously! This is the wisdom of such organizations as BNI International.

Remember this: *Networking is not a "one-way street."* Those who are good at networking both give and receive help. Hence, networking is a "two-way street." I never take help from anyone without thinking about how I can return the favor. There is nothing worse than the person who takes and takes and takes, but never gives anything back in return.

Christopher Michel, CEO of Military.com, said, "Good networking is not a one-time activity; it is about staying in touch, providing value to your contacts, and giving back. The sincerity of your relationships matter—no one wants to hear from you only when you need something. If you start networking in conjunction with your business development, you already are behind the power curve. The best networkers do not see networking as a shortcut to business startup—they thrive on connecting with people, helping others, and staying in touch throughout their lives."

In today's world, selfishness is rampant. Instead of dishing out goods to others, many people dish out nothing but negativism and stab each other in the back. I would never want a person in my network who has continually worked to stab me in the back. I would never consider these people as part of my network, and would never help them to get ahead.

Think about whom you can help. You may be surprised that some will give back to you much more than you will have ever given to them. These people are the ones you want to cultivate as important nodes in your network.

Why Network?

If you want to get ahead in business, you must network. If you want a good job, network. If you want raises, network. If you want promotions, network. If you want to receive awards and recognition, network. If you want choice assignments, network. If you want to meet people, network. If you want help, network. If you want to help others, network. And most of all, if you want an overabundance of clients, network.

Networking Is the Hottest Thing to Do

Networking is one of the hottest things to do in business development. Everyone thinks networking is the next best thing to sliced bread. And it is! However, do not overdo it. You only have twenty-four hours in a day. So, do not make a point to see or talk to every Tom, Dick, Harry, and GI Joe that crosses your path. Do not attend every job fair or conference. Do not attend every professional organizational meeting or business-networking meeting. If you did all of these things to the exclusion of other necessary activities, you would be wasting a lot of your valuable time.

Susan Wilson Solovic, CEO of Small Business Television (www.sbtv.com) said, "Effective networking is time-consuming, and you may think that you're too busy managing your home, family, or business to find time. But, if your goal is to have success and power, you can't afford not to network. You never know when you'll meet someone who will be instrumental in helping you to achieve your goals."

Build a Network

Build a network of people who provide mutual help. This is the most productive use of your time. However, there is a method to this madness. You must network smartly. Do not network for the sake of networking, but network for positive, constructive results. If you do not achieve good results, you are not networking effectively.

Build a network and achieve the following:
- Build a network of people who provide mutual help.
- Develop a wide network of friends and collaborators.

- Develop a fine-tuned network of mutual, complementary job-searching peers and helpers.
- Attend networking meetings and events.
- Cultivate good job references through your network.
- Join ClubNet (Job Club) and participate in professional networking.
- Network through the deans of your college.
- Network with friends of a friend.

Fallacy: "Network with Everybody and Anybody"

You can waste more of your valuable time following this bad advice. Judy Rosemarin, founder of Sense-Able Strategies wrote, "Networking doesn't mean making thousands of contacts. Instead, write provocative letters introducing yourself, then arrange ways to discuss mutually interesting subjects with a few key people. If you view your search as a personal research project on a compelling subject—your own future—you'll find it easier to collect critical information and ideas."

As the broader base of your business network triangle increases, the number of people you need to speak with to reach the right decision makers increases. Hence, the time it takes to reach the key decision makers increases.

You do not have enough hours in the day to talk with everyone. This is why it is not such a good idea to speak with every neighbor, postal delivery person, milkman, yardman, church member, door-to-door solicitor, friend, relative, former employee, classmate, and stranger in the marketplace. They may all be well intentioned, but are not connected to the apex of your business network triangle. Hence, *you need to be judicious about whom you talk to in your networking activities.*

It is more productive and effective to talk to people in your industry who know of business openings in their companies and within their networks. This approach enhances your focus and effectiveness, and further increases your odds of finding the clients you are seeking. A side benefit is that you can validate your value, experience, and credentials with those in the know within the industry of today's business market.

The Best Route to Find Clients

I think one of the best sources of clients are the references you have already cultivated in your network. The references are your contact points. Develop those nodes. I acquired consulting jobs because of networking. I obtained most of my regular projects through networking. *Networking is the best source to find business and employment.* Hence, start developing your network by developing good references.

Look for about five companies that you really want to perform work for and do the due diligence on these companies. Gather information, develop contacts, and keep up with the companies. Gather information from each company's Web site. Try to "break in" to meet and chat with employees within those companies.

Continue to develop your skills and experience that every business wants. Here is the best route:

- **Prospectus.** Continue to "beef up" and polish your company prospectus and executive summary.

- **Organizations.** Join a professional organization or two in your career area of choice and place them in your prospectus.

- **Service.** Get involved in serving on committees, run for office, and participate in meetings of these professional organizations.

- **Education.** Take additional courses and certifications in your business area of choice that you can add to your prospectus.

- **Bullets.** Continue to do great things at your present internship or job to develop good bullets to add to your prospectus.

- **Meetings.** Attend conferences, seminars, workshops, and trade shows in your business area of choice.

- **Papers.** Prepare papers for presenting at these conferences and publishing in their periodicals.

- **Articles.** Write articles to be published in these professional organization periodicals.

- **Book.** Write a book on your business area of interest and get it published.

If you do these things, you will have a dynamite prospectus and executive summary. You will receive many calls for work. You will perform well in negotiations and obtain several clients. You will be able to negotiate the best deal you can get with every offer. You will be able to leverage one offer against another to maximize your final offer and project. You will be able to prepare more "beefy" summaries for each new project you secure. The process will continue ad infinitum.

The Best Way to Break into any Company

The best way to break into any company is to have someone on the inside working to get you in. This is why networking is one of the most important strategies for seeking a good job. If it were not for networking, I would not have obtained most of my jobs. I would not have been on the consulting gigs I acquired if it were not for networking. Take maximum advantage of networking.

How Should I Network?

There are many ways to network. You can network in person. You can network on the phone. You can network with e-mails. You can network with letters (or snail mail). You can network using fax messages. You can network using text messaging on your BlackBerry. You can network on the Internet. You can network using teleconferencing, videoconferencing, and Web cameras on your laptop. You can network in chat rooms. You can network in Web logs (or blogs). The list goes on and on.

Networking Methods

What methods can be used for networking? In summary, some of the methods that can be used to network and communicate are as follows:

- Talking face-to-face in meetings and/or interviews
- Talking by telephone one-on-one and by conference call
- Writing and sending letters/memos/cards by snail mail
- Preparing, sending, and receiving faxes
- Writing, sending, and receiving e-mail through the Internet
- Talking through teleconferencing, videoconferencing, and Web cameras
- Communicating through text messages on Palm Pilots, BlackBerries, and cell phones
- Communicating through chat rooms, Web logs (blogs), and instant messaging

Networking Lists

It is not bad if three of your networking colleagues are from where you work. The most important criterion is whether your networking colleagues are quality references. In other words, you can effectively communicate with and maintain throughout your career only a limited number of networking contacts. Hence, it is very important that your contacts are quality contacts ... those you help and vice versa.

You can have an endless list of networking colleagues, but you will want to cultivate and maintain only about ten of them as quality contacts throughout your career and lifetime. These are the people whom you trust implicitly, meet with periodically, keep in touch with by phone/e-mail throughout your career, and mutually depend on helping with letters of reference and job references.

Make your list as detailed as necessary for it to be effective in helping you in the future. Remember this: If networking is only a one-way affair, it is for naught. It must be a mutually beneficial relationship.

Phone Calling

When I was laid off once before, I remember spending hours and hours on the telephone at the career center cold-calling everyone I knew, company after company. You know? It was a grand waste of time. I learned that the hard way.

Our job consultant told us that networking was the best thing to do and to call everyone on our contact list. Well, I did just that, and it was a huge waste of my valuable time. Telephoning for the sake of telephoning is not very productive.

Instead, find those individuals who can provide you with good leads, advice, and help. They are the ones with whom you want to spend your time on the phone. Do strategic phoning, not telemarketing. People hate telemarketing and telemarketers.

Make your phone calls work for you. You have more important things to do than just "shoot the bull" with friends and relatives across the country. Do you realize that some people actually do that? Because they can use the career center phones for free, they call all of their friends and relatives throughout the country just to chitchat. What a waste of time ... not to mention taxpayers' money!

Make Your Calls Count

Every person is predominantly either a talker or a writer. If orally oriented, you would probably prefer to network face-to-face in person or by phone instead of by e-mail. Making phone calls is good, but just making phone calls for the sake of making phone calls is not good. Cold-calling is a waste of time. We must focus on making calls to the right people in the right places at the right time.

In a CareerJournal.com article, Perri Capell said, "Perhaps it's not just lack of time that's holding you back, but lack of confidence. It's unnerving to make calls when you doubt the person you're about to contact wants to hear from you.

However, when that nice e-mail comes back, the anxiety melts away. Take some time and try it."

Since the advent of voice mail, one of the real drawbacks of using the telephone is that people will only return calls to callers with whom they want to speak. The pervasive telemarketing industry has soured many people in returning calls to names of people and/or phone numbers they do not readily recognize. Additionally, people are so busy these days that it is extremely difficult to get them to answer the phone the moment you call. You could play "phone tag" for days on end, which wastes a lot of your valuable time.

Hence, if you prefer to network by phone, develop a list of names, titles, companies, and phone numbers of the right selection of people to call. Make at least ten to fifteen calls per day. From these calls, you may generate one to two great leads for opportunities. If you do not make ten to fifteen calls a day, you will not build up a head of steam and keep the momentum going.

Another point in phone networking is to:

- Make a call.
- Follow it with an e-mail.
- Follow the e-mail with a follow-up call.

If you receive no response, go on to the next contact. In your phone conversation, do not come across as being desperate.

Refrain from making repeated calls or queries to someone who neither returns your calls nor responds to your e-mails. In other words, do not be a pest. There is a fine line between being persistent and being a pest. You do not want to be a pest, particularly if the person you are calling is actively avoiding you. If he does not want to speak with you, chances are he will not hire you. So, why waste your time?

Networking at Relevant Places and Events

Let us look at what could be considered relevant networking places and events. These are some examples of places and events where you can network with relevant people:

- Job networking meetings or gatherings
- Career or job classes, courses, and seminars
- Technical conventions
- Trade shows
- Professional organizational meetings

- Job or career shows and fairs
- Career or job centers
- Company open houses with potential work for you
- Small Business Administration (SBA) events
- Better Business Bureau networking events

Attend strategically selected professional networking groups and professional society chapter meetings. These groups and meetings provide a wealth of resources and often lead to credible contacts and leads for business and job opportunities. Participating in these networking groups raises your awareness on industry issues and job-search challenges. Because you are involved with peers with similar career and business directions, they may offer volunteer opportunities specifically related to your goals.

We keep hearing that the best way to find an executive job is through networking. However, not everyone knows how to network effectively or has good contacts to mine. This may explain the allure of structured networking groups—organizations that schedule meetings and other opportunities for members to connect and share job leads with the help of facilitators.

Some of the national and regional organizations offering structured networking events are as follows:

- ExecuNet—www.execunet.com
- The Five O'Clock Club—www.fiveoclockclub.com
- The Financial Executives Networking Group—www.thefeng.org
- Technology Executives Networking Group—www.theteng.org
- Forty Plus—www.fortyplus.org
- BNI International—www.bni.com

These get-togethers range from informal meetings to formal programs with prescribed reading or coursework. The groups offering them may be for-profit, not-for-profit, or state-sponsored. Defined by profession, income level, geography, demographic, or some combination of these factors, they seek to make job hunters comfortable with networking. Networking organizations may offer other assistance as well and charge higher membership fees to provide it. However, the group-networking events tend to be affordable—in the $30 to $45 range—and their organizers stress that everyone participates.

Be prepared to be sized up when you step into the networking scene. Here's a quick list to help you stand up to the scrutiny:

- Dress appropriate to the venue. If the event is at a person's home, a three-piece suit is probably not required.

- Practice your handshake. Firm—not abusive.

- Pop a breath mint—or two.

- Do not be overbearing. As strange as it seems, some people attend these events to unwind. The strong sell won't work.

- Take plenty of business cards.

However, do not overdo networking at these events. You have many other important activities to spend your valuable time doing in your twenty-four-hour day to build your business. So, strike a good, happy balance.

Less Productive Places and Events

There are other places and events where networking can be done, but they generally are not as productive as those mentioned above because they are not specifically related to building business, they are usually not companies with which you could work, and work-related topics are not often discussed there. Examples of some of these less productive places and events include:

- Church
- Grocery store, drug store, and other stores
- Barber shop
- Walking on the street/sidewalks
- While in a taxi or cab
- Attending a non-job-related social function
- Movie theater
- Sporting event
- Restaurants
- Visiting companies that are not in your career field
- Gas stations

By a fluke, you could meet someone at these places and events. However, the amount of time spent networking at these locations will not be as productive as the time spent at the locations mentioned first. Therefore, be choosy in selecting the places and events where you spend your time networking.

Perri Capell of CareerJournal.com said, "If you're doing it right, networking isn't something that takes lots of extra time in your life. It easily blends into your life and your approach to life."

Finer Points of Networking

We have covered some of the more basic approaches to networking in the previous sections of this chapter. The following section covers some of the finer points of networking such as traps, silence, slobs, strategic networking, and hard-to-find information.

Networking Traps to Guard Against

Douglas Richardson, author of *Savvy Job Hunters Learn to Network Nicely,* said, "Networking is still the most effective job-search and self-marketing tool, but when done ineptly, it's also the most obnoxious. Many job hunters blunder through the process, causing potential employers and contacts to feel misused and manipulated."

Networking is being packaged as a canned, impersonal, and manipulative technique. As a result, a lot of bad networking occurs. Many networking contacts are feeling used and abused, and the abusers are poisoning the well for others. Regardless of what the process is called, humans will always help each other unless their efforts are demeaned and unreciprocated. Job seekers who ignore this truth deserve the hostility they receive.

Networking and Awkward Silence

Never let the conversation get to a point of an awkward silence. As soon as you complete what you need to say after a brief conversation, just say, "It was nice meeting you, and I hope to see you again." Shake hands, smile, and depart. Just make it a smooth transition.

Remember this: When a conversation comes to an awkward silence, I assure you, both parties feel uncomfortable. Hence, do not let your conversation get to that point. Close and depart at the peak of the upswing, not at the bottom of the downswing.

Slobs Will Not Get the Good Jobs

I looked at some of the photographs that were posted on a Web site showing job fairs. I was totally amazed and appalled to see that most of the students who visited the booths were dressed like total slobs. If they were expecting to make a bad impression on the recruiters and really didn't want a job, then they were dressed exactly right for that job fair. If you are applying for a laborer or outside job, then it is probably appropriate to dress down. However, if you are applying for a professional job working inside, or searching for business contacts and clients, then I suggest you dress in a more presentable manner.

You attend these job fairs to network. When you network with a company you would like to do work for, you should dress in a manner that would impress instead of depress those staffing the booth. The recruiters at these booths are usually dressed pretty well. Why? Because they are trying to impress you! What makes these students feel that they are in such great demand that they too don't need to dress appropriately to impress the recruiters? As a business owner, you must set the standard and image for your company.

It is better to be overdressed than underdressed.

If I were hiring people for a job or to consult on a project (and I have hired many people in my career), I would not hire anyone looking like a slob. What is the reason for that? It is because they, in all probability, will perform the work on the job the same way ... as slobs. Their work will be sloppy. Their office will look sloppy. They will present a sloppy image to our customers. That's why!

Remember this: Slobs will not get the good jobs or contracts. Dress is very important. Dress appropriately to make a good impression. Do it right!

Strategic Networking

Networking is the most important of all of your strategies for capturing business or a good job. People acquire most good jobs through effective networking. Do a lot of networking, but limit it to strategic networking. Network with those contacts you want to cultivate and keep on your networking matrix. You can find opportunities through your good contacts in your network.

Remember, whenever any of your networking contacts does something for you, you should feel obligated to return the favor and do something for him or her. Networking is a two-way street. It is an "If you'll scratch my back, I'll scratch your back" arrangement. Lawyers call that a quid pro quo arrangement.

"Networking should be viewed as a business transaction," says Douglas Richardson in *Why Women Make Better Networkers*, "which drives a specialized economy of favors. The deal is, if I give you a favor, you owe me a favor." Each exchange of favors is supposed to preserve a mutually advantageous system of informal communication, not establish an interpersonal relationship, he says. Moreover, both sides must hold up their end for the system to remain healthy.

Moral of the story is, if you want the business, bend over backward to appease the contact.

Strategically Network with High-Value People

Do strategic networking. In other words, pick high-value people with whom to network. What I mean here by "high-value" people are not necessarily high-ranking executives. I mean those people who can give you business, get you business, or influence someone to give you business. Spend your time networking with those high-value people.

The number of networking, professional association, civic, and charitable group events held in any given week can be overwhelming. Don't drive yourself crazy trying to hit them all—be smart. Carefully select the events that you believe are the best fit for you personally and professionally.

How to Obtain Hard-To-Find Information

Make a list of the kinds of sources and methods for acquiring intelligence or information that would help you reach a truer understanding of the corporate culture of a company. Some information may appear to be unobtainable. However, where there is a will, there is way. Of course, readily available information is easy to obtain from the following open sources:

- Library, databases, info banks, and repositories
- Internet (company Web sites, stock market Web sites, Web-news sites, and search engines)
- Articles in newspapers, magazines, journals, and other publications
- News reports (radio, television, and Internet)
- Company brochures, fliers, reports, and collateral
- Annual reports, 10K reports, and Dun & Bradstreet reports
- Conferences, seminars, workshops, conventions, trade shows, and meetings
- Industry sources of reference materials
- Career centers
- Your network of friends
- Any other open literature or sources

The next level of information is from knowledgeable sources including the following:

- Knowledgeable people in the industry (headhunters, recruiters, employment agencies, consultants, researchers, and career coaches)
- Current company employees whom you know (close friends in the company, someone you meet casually, and cold-called employees)
- Disgruntled current company employees [**best sources**]
- Former employees—those who quit, got fired, laid off, etc. [**best sources**]
- People working in human resources, finance, security, and administration

Where there is a will, there is a way to find out anything and everything you want to know and use.

Remember this: It is not what you know that counts. It is not even who you know that counts. However, what really counts is what you know of who you know.

Conclusion

Networking is the most important technique for finding business and for rapidly building your business. Hone your networking skills and you will be successful in all of your business endeavors.

Baseball is the only major sport in which the defensive team initiates the action. The game does not start until the ball is delivered from the pitcher. Offense begins by stepping up to the plate. When you think about it, the same is true when networking for a new position. To reach contacts and secure referrals, you must step into the batter's box. You may strike out at first, but eventually you'll hit a home run that leads to the business you want.

Do not lose heart if you step up to the plate, swing, and miss—repeatedly. Striking out is part of the game, but sitting on the bench means watching the game go by. Remember that baseball's leading hitters make successful contact only three times out of ten. They also step up to the plate more than five hundred times a year.

Years ago, an entrepreneur had a similar experience. To finance his dream project, he visited 301 banks, which all denied his request for capital. But, an officer at the 302nd bank said, "Okay, we'll help you build your theme park, Mr. Disney." Perseverance paid off for Walt Disney and will pay off for you as well.

Even if it doesn't come naturally, networking is an art that can be learned. You do not have to be inherently gregarious and outgoing. Just have a genuine curiosity and interest in others. The result can be personally and professionally rewarding.

It is extremely important for you to recruit a good mentor. You need someone who is objective and who will give you frank, no-holds-barred advice and suggestions for improvement. Your mentor can look at your business and give you pointers for improvement. He can give you ideas on how to find business effectively, and validate your search strategies, tactics, and assumptions. Finally, your mentor can help you to gain a broader perspective in your business field.

Afterword

When I was ten years old, I started my first entrepreneurial venture, Dave's Landscaping Service. This developed by networking with my next-door neighbor, who was about to give up a lawn-cutting job at another neighbor's house. I wanted that job so badly, I could taste it. And even better, it paid a whopping $3.00. Mind you, this was 1972.

The neighbor whose lawn I was going to be cutting was a bit skeptical because of my age. This was the first time I had ever faced a situation like this. To maneuver around my age factor, when talking to the neighbor I simply pointed to my backyard and the beautiful condition the grass was in. I mentioned to my neighbor that I always helped my father take care of the lawn, which was beautiful.

My dad, always the perfectionist, has prided himself on the condition of our lawn for as long as I can remember. It is the greenest grass around, and our flowers bloom longer than anyone else's. People walking by our house would mention that it was the best-looking lawn around. Lucky for me, the basement in our house always had a wide assortment of extra lawn and plant fertilizer, rakes, shovels, and every other yard tool known to mankind.

I can remember when I pointed to my yard, while talking with the neighbor, and mentioned that my dad had passed all of his lawn "secrets" along to me and that I would have their lawn looking shipshape in no time. The neighbor was hooked!

I tirelessly mowed that lawn every week, spread a little fertilizer on it, and raked it in the autumn. The next year, my neighbor passed my name along to her sister who lived in the next town and was looking for a lawn service. Dave's Landscaping Service to the rescue. This was my first run-in with word-of-mouth advertisement. Every Saturday morning, I would either ride my bicycle the four or five miles to my second lawn job, or if my Dad was free, he would drive me. This lawn was a lot bigger than the other, so I charged $10.00 to cut it. In the fall, I hated that yard because now I had to rake the leaves. However, I was able to charge $20.00–$25.00, so my hatred quickly disappeared when I was paid.

By the end of my second year in business, I was making more than any other kid at school and had lawns all over town. Through word-of-mouth advertisement, networking with other kids and taking over lawns they no longer wanted, and my leveraging the good-looking backyard at my house, my life as an entrepreneur was taking off.

I can remember sitting in my school classes daydreaming about building the biggest lawn service business around and writing out my first business and marketing plan. Usually, due to my mind wandering, I would often be scolded by my teachers for not paying attention in class. It was not until my adult years that I learned I shared my love of entrepreneurial daydreaming with many billionaire entrepreneurs. They too were scolded in school for not paying attention.

When I decided to teach university courses, coach business owners, and start a consulting business, I was able to pick up contracts worth over $100,000 very quickly. I was able to do this by using the same formula I learned at age ten.

I have since grown my coaching and consulting business to include clients all over the world, while also starting a Web services business and a publishing and speaking venture. With every entrepreneurial startup I begin, I always turn to my business success system that I started at age ten. It is that formula that makes up the strategies in this book.

Like so many entrepreneurs before me, I am a student of the business world. I devour every book, magazine, and Web site I can find to help me continually feed my thirst for cutting-edge, business-building information. I pass this extra strategy on to you, the up-and-coming entrepreneur. Become an expert in your chosen business industry, network feverishly, publish articles, speak to whoever will listen, and become a student of the entrepreneurial masters.

By following this formula for business success, just as a ten-year-old boy did, you will not only plan and pave a path for your own success, you will also become a High-Performance Entrepreneur!

Appendix A: Information Resources

One of the most serious mistakes made by startup entrepreneurs is not seeking out help from available resources. Trying to do it "My Way" only works in songs, not in business. You should seek out and find the resources that are applicable to your needs. Below is a good list to start from as sources of information.

American Bar Association Service Center
www.abanet.org
321 North Clark Street
Chicago, IL 60610
(800) 285-2221

ASAE Directory of Associations Online
www.asaecenter.org

About.com's E-Commerce 101
http://onlinebusiness.about.com/cs/startingup/a/101.htm

Better Business Bureau
www.bbb.org

Business Owner's Tool Kit
www.toolkit.cch.com
Endless amounts of great business information.

Center for Business Women's Research
www.womensbusinessresearch.org/index.asp

Chamber of Commerce Small Business Center
www.uschamber.com/sb/default

Consumer Response Center
Federal Trade Commission—Rm. 130
600 Pennsylvania Ave. NW
Washington, DC 20580

Dunn & Bradstreet's Small Business Solutions
http://smallbusiness.dnb.com

Economic Statistics and Research
www.sba.gov/advo/research

Equifax
www.equifax.com
Credit Reports

Experian
www.experian.com
Credit Reports

FRANDATA Corporation
www.frandata.com
1665 North Fort Meyer Dr., Suite 410
Arlington, VA 22209
(703) 740-4707

FranchiseHelp, Inc.
www.franchisehelp.com
101 Executive Boulevard, 2nd Floor
Elmsford, NY 10523
(800) 401-1446

Franchise-Insider.com
www.franchise-insider.com
745 Campbell Way
Herndon, VA 20170
(877) 674-6677

Freedom of Information Act Request
Federal Trade Commission
Washington, DC 20580
Identify your letter as a "FOIA Request" and include (1) your name, address, and daytime phone number, and (2) the name and address of the company you are asking about.

Internet Public Library
www.ipl.org

North American Securities Administrators Association
www.nasaa.org/Industry_Regulatory_Resources/Uniform_Forms/
750 First Street, Suite 710
Washington, DC 20002
(202) 737-0900

National Small Business Development Centers (SBDC)
www.sba.gov/sbdc
By location (your backyard local)—all-inclusive, free business guidance

Population Studies and Training Center's Population and Demography Resources
www.pstc.brown.edu

Service Corps of Retired Executives (SCORE)
www.score.org
National organization sponsored by SBA of over 13,000 volunteer business executives who provide free counseling, workshops, and seminars to prospective and existing small business people.

Small Business Development Center (SBDC)
http://sbdcnet.org/
Sponsored by the SBA in partnership with state and local governments, the educational community, and the private sector. They provide assistance, counseling, and training to prospective and existing business people.

Small Business Development Center Net Industry Information
http://sbdcnet.org/industry.php

The Veterans Corporation (Vetcorp)
www.veteranscorp.org
TVC provides veterans with the tools and resources they need to be successful in business: access to capital, access to business services, entrepreneurial education, surety bonding, insurance and prescription coverage, and veterans business directory.

Trade Associations
www.fita.org

TransUnion
www.transunion.com
Credit Reports

Veterans' Business Outreach Center
www.vboc.org
The Veterans' Business Outreach Center provides business training, counseling, technical assistance, and mentoring to veterans, reservist, national guard, and active-duty business owners and startup candidates in the Southeast region of the United States.

U.S. Government Resources

Agriculture (USDA)
www.usda.gov
12th Street and Independence Avenue, SW
Washington, DC 20250

The USDA offers publications on selling to the USDA. Publications and programs on entrepreneurship are also available through county extension offices nationwide.

U.S. Business Advisor
www.business.gov
The official business link to the U.S. government is managed by the U.S. Small Business Administration (SBA) in partnership with twenty-one other federal agencies. This partnership, known as Business Gateway, is a presidential e-government initiative that provides a single access point to government services and information to help the nation's businesses with their operations.

Center for Veterans Enterprise (CVE)
www.vetbiz.gov
Designed to assist veteran entrepreneurs who want to start and expand their businesses in the federal and private marketplace.

Department of Commerce (DOC)
www.commerce.gov
Office of Business Liaison
14th Street and Constitution Avenue NW
Room 5898C
Washington, DC 20230
DOC's Business Assistance Center provides listings of business opportunities available in the federal government. This service also will refer businesses to different programs and services in the DOC and other federal agencies.

Consumer Information Center (CIC)
www.pueblo.gsa.gov
PO Box 100
Pueblo, CO 81002
The CIC offers a consumer information catalog of federal publications.

Government Small Business Publications

Many federal agencies offer publications of interest to small businesses. There is a nominal fee for some, but most are free. Below is a selected list of government agencies that provide publications and other services targeted to small businesses. To receive their publications, contact the regional offices listed in the telephone directory or write to the addresses below.

Consumer Product Safety Commission (CPSC)
www.cpsc.gov
Publications Request
Washington, DC 20207
The CPSC offers guidelines for product safety requirements.

Environmental Protection Agency (EPA)
www.epa.gov
The EPA offers more than one hundred publications designed to help small businesses understand how they can comply with EPA regulations.

Small Business Ombudsman
401 M Street SW (A-149C)
Washington, DC 20460
1-800-368-5888 except DC and VA
(703) 557-1938 in DC and VA

FirstGov

www.USA.gov

Whatever you want or need from the U.S. government, it is here on FirstGov. You will find a rich treasure of online information, services, and resources.

FedStats

www.fedstats.gov

Various federal agencies collecting statistics.

Food and Drug Administration (FDA)

www.fda.gov

FDA Center for Food Safety and Applied Nutrition

200 Charles Street SW

Washington, DC 20402

The FDA offers information on packaging and labeling requirements for food and food-related products.

Grants

www.grants.gov

Find and apply for federal government grants. There are over a thousand grant programs offered by all federal grant-making agencies.

Government Loans

www.govloans.gov

Resource for all government benefits and includes information on hundreds of benefit programs. To find additional benefit and assistance programs, visit www. GovBenefits.gov.

Government Printing Office

www.gpo.gov

Many publications on business management and other related topics are available from the Government Printing Office (GPO). GPO bookstores are located in twenty-four major cities and are listed in the Yellow Pages under the bookstore heading. You can request a Subject Bibliography by writing to Government Printing Office, Superintendent of Documents, Washington, DC 20402-9328.

Internal Revenue Service (IRS)

www.irs.gov

Labor (DOL)
www.dol.gov
Employment Standards Administration
200 Constitution Avenue NW
Washington, DC 20210
The DOL offers publications on compliance with labor laws.

Labor (reemployment issues)
www.dol.gov/elaws/userra.htm

Labor, Veterans' Employment and Training Services
www.dol.gov/vets

Library of Congress Ask a Librarian
www.loc.gov/rr/askalib

Small Business Administration (SBA)
www.sba.gov
The SBA offers an extensive selection of information on most business management topics, from how to start a business to exporting your products. This information is listed in *The Small Business Directory*. For a free copy, contact your nearest SBA office. SBA has offices throughout the country. Consult the U.S. government section in your telephone directory for the office nearest you. SBA offers a number of programs and services, including training and educational programs, counseling services, financial programs, and contract assistance.

SBA Office of Advocacy
www.sba.gov/advo/
Office of Advocacy is the voice for small business in the federal government.

SBA Office of Economic Research
www.sba.gov/advo/research/
Small business research and statistics, economic research, policy analyses, and small business outreach.

SBA Veterans Lending Programs
www.sba.gov/vets/lending.html

SBA Services to Help Veterans Succeed in Business
www.sba.gov/vets
Anything and everything for the veteran who is thinking about starting a business or is in business.

Treasury
www.irs.gov
Internal Revenue Service (IRS)
PO Box 25866
Richmond, VA 23260
1-800-424-3676
The IRS offers information on tax requirements for small businesses.

Veterans Affairs
www.va.gov

Reference Manuals

Dot Com Disclosures (Information about Online Advertising)
www.ftc.gov/bcp/conline/pubs/buspubs/dotcom/index.shtml
An FTC staff paper that provides additional information for online advertisers.

IRS Employment Taxes for Small Businesses
www.IRS.gov.

Franchise Registry
www.franchiseregistry.com/

Franchise Directories and Evaluation
http://sbdcnet.org/SBIC/franchise.php

How Business Structure Affects Business Names
www.toolkit.cch.com/text/P01_4800.asp

Starting a Business and Keeping Records
www.irs.gov/publications/p583/index.html

Small Business Development Center E-Commerce Guide
http://sbdcnet.org/SBIC/e-com.php

Trademark FAQs
www.uspto.gov/web/offices/tac/tmfaq.htm

American Society of Association Executives
www.asaecenter.org

Marketing Resource Center
www.marketingsource.com
By using their interactive keyword search capabilities, you can search through over 35,000 associations and organizations that cover almost every type of business imaginable.

Training Courses

HiPer Solutions
www.hipercoaching.com
Business startup teleclasses, seminars, and a great selection of resources.

Network of Training and Counseling Services
www.sba.gov/ed/
Find free training on business development, business plans, management issues, accounting, funding, and many more.

SBA
www.sba.gov/training/courses.html

SCORE
www.score.org/business

Vetcorp
catalog.veteranscorp.org/catalog/index

Appendix B: Small Business Development Center Directory

Look to your local SBDC to provide you with free business startup consulting.

Alabama
University of Alabama—Birmingham
1500 1st Avenue North, R118
Birmingham, AL 35203
Phone: 205-307-6510
Fax: 205-307-6511
Web site: www.asbdc.org

Alaska
University of Alaska—Anchorage
430 West Seventh Avenue, Suite 110
Anchorage, AK 99501-3550
Phone: 907-274-7232
Fax: 907-274-9524
Web site: www.aksbdc.org

American Samoa
American Samoa Community College
PO Box 2609
Pago Pago, American Samoa 96799
Phone: 011-684-699-4830
Fax: 011-684-699-6132
Web site: www.as-sbdc.org

Arizona
Arizona Small Business Development Center Network
Maricopa County Community College
2411 West 14th Street, Suite 114
Tempe, AZ 85281
Phone: 480-731-8722
Fax: 480-731-8729
Web site: www.azsbdc.net/Default.aspx

Arkansas

University of Arkansas at Little Rock
2801 South University Avenue, Rm. 260
Little Rock, AR 72204
Phone: 501-683-7700
Fax: 501-683-7720
Web site: www.asbdc.ualr.edu

California

Fresno
University of California—Merced
550 East Shaw, Suite 100
Fresno, CA 93710-7702
Phone: 559-241-6590
Fax: 559-241-7422
Web site: http://sbdc.ucmerced.edu

Los Angeles Region
Long Beach Community College District
3950 Paramount Boulevard, Ste. 101
Lakewood, CA 90712
Phone: 562-938-5004
Fax: 562-938-5030
Web site: www.lasbdcnet.ibcc.edu/lead.html

Sacramento
California State University—Chico
35 Main Street, Room 203
Chico, CA 95929-0765
Phone: 530-898-4598
Fax: 530-898-4734
Web site: www.csuchico.edu/cedp/

San Diego
Southwestern Community College District
900 Otay Lakes Road, Bldg. 1681
Chula Vista, CA 91910-7299
Phone: 619-482-6388
Fax: 619-482-6402
Web site: www.sbditc.org

Francisco
Humboldt State University
Office of Economic Development
1 Harpst Street
Arcata, CA 95521
Phone: 707-826-3920
Web site: www.norcalsbdc.org

Santa Ana
California State University—Fullerton
800 North State College Boulevard, LH640
Fullerton, CA 92834
Phone: 714-278-2719
Fax: 714-278-7858
Web site: www.leadsbdc.org

Colorado
Office of Economic Development
1625 Broadway, Suite 2700
Denver, CO 80202
Phone: 303-892-3864
Fax: 303-892-3848
Web site: www.coloradosbdc.org

Connecticut
University of Central Connecticut
185 Main Street
New Britain, CT 06051
Phone: 860-827-7104
Fax: 860-827-7112
Web site: www.ccsu.edu/itbd

Delaware
Delaware Technology Park
1 Innovation Way, Suite 301
Newark, DE 19711
Phone: 302-831-1555
Fax: 302-831-1423
Web site: www.delawaresbdc.org

District of Columbia
Howard University School of Business
2600 6th Street NW, Room 128
Washington, DC 20059
Phone: 202-806-1550
Fax: 202-806-1777
Web site: www.dcsbdc.com/

Florida
University of West Florida
401 East Chase Street, Suite 100
Pensacola, FL 32502-6160
Phone: 850-473-7800
Fax: 850-473-7813
Web site: www.floridasbdc.coM

Georgia
University of Georgia
1180 East Broad Street
Athens, GA 30602-5412
Phone: 706-542-2762
Fax: 706-542-7935
Web site: www.georgiasbdc.org

Guam
University of Guam
Pacific Islands SBDC
PO Box 5014—U.O.G. Station Mangilao
Mangilao, GU 96923
Phone: 671-735-2590
Fax: 671-734-2002
Web site: www.pacificsbdc.com

Hawaii
University of Hawaii—Hilo
308 Kamehameha Avenue, Suite 201
Hilo, HI 96720-2960
Phone: 808-974-7515
Fax: 808-974-7683
Web site: www.hawaii-sbdc.org

Idaho
Boise State University
1910 University Drive
Boise, ID 83725-1655
Phone: 208-426-3799
Fax: 208-426-3877
Web site: www.idahosbdc.org

Illinois
Department of Commerce and Economic Opportunity
620 East Adams Street, 4th Floor
Springfield, IL 62701-1615
Phone: 217-524-5700
Fax: 217-524-0171
Web site: www.ilsbdc.biz

Indiana
Indiana Economic Development Corporation
One North Capitol, Suite 900
Indianapolis, IN 46204-2043
Phone: 317-234-2086
Fax: 317-232-8872
Web site: www.isbdc.org

Iowa
Iowa State University
340 Gerdin Business Bldg.
Ames, IA 50011-1350
Phone: 515-294-2030
Fax: 515-294-6522
Web site: www.iowasbdc.org

Kansas
Fort Hays State University
214 SW Sixth Street, Suite 301
Topeka, KS 66603-3719
Phone: 785-296-6514
Fax: 785-291-3261
Web site: www.fhsu.edu/ksbdc

Kentucky

University of Kentucky
225 Gatton College of Business Economics Building
Lexington, KY 40506-0034
Phone: 859-257-7668
Fax: 859-323-1907
Web site: www.ksbdc.org

Louisiana

University of Louisiana—Monroe
College of Business Administration
700 University Avenue
Monroe, LA 71209-6435
Phone: 318-342-5506
Fax: 318-342-5510
Web site: www.lsbdc.org

Maine

University of Southern Maine
96 Falmouth Street
PO Box 9300
Portland, ME 04103-9300
Phone: 207-780-4420
Fax: 207-780-4810
Web site: www.mainesbdc.org

Maryland

University of Maryland
7100 Baltimore Avenue, Suite 401
College Park, MD 20740-3640
Phone: 301-403-8300 x 15
Fax: 301-403-8303
Web site: www.mdsbdc.umd.edu

Massachusetts

University of Massachusetts
227 Isenberg School of Management
121 President's Drive
Amherst, MA 01003-9310

Phone: 413-545-6301
Fax: 413-545-1273
Web site: www.msbdc.org/

Michigan
Grand Valley State University
510 West Fulton Avenue
Grand Rapids, MI 49504
Phone: 616-331-7480
Fax: 616-331-7385
Web site: www.misbtdc.org

Minnesota
Minnesota Small Business Development Center
1st National Bank Building
332 Minnesota Street, Suite E200
St. Paul, MN 55101-1351
Phone: 651-297-5770
Fax: 651-296-5287
Web site: www.mnsbdc.com

Mississippi
University of Mississippi
B-19 Jeanette Phillips Drive
PO Box 1848
University, MS 38677-1848
Phone: 662-915-5001
Fax: 662-915-5650
Web site: www.mssbdc.org

Missouri
University of Missouri
410 S. Sixth St.
200 Engineering North
Columbia, MO 65211
Phone: 573-882-0344
Fax: 573-884-4297
Web site: www.missouribusiness.net/sbdc/

Montana
Department of Commerce
301 South Park Avenue, Room 116/PO Box 200505
Helena, MT 59601
Phone: 406-841-27468
Fax: 406-841-2728
Web site: http://sbdc.mt.gov/

Nebraska
University of Nebraska—Omaha
415 Roskens Hall
6001 Dodge Street
Omaha, NE 68182-0248
Phone: 402-554-2521
Fax: 402-554-3473
Web site: http://nbdc.unomaha.edu

Nevada
University of Nevada—Reno
Reno College of Business
Nazir Ansari Bldg. 032, Rm. 4
Reno, NV 89557-0100
Phone: 775-784-1717
Fax: 775-784-4337
Web site: www.nsbdc.org

New Hampshire
University of New Hampshire
Mittemore School of Business and Economics, UNH
110 McConnell Hall
Durham, NH 03824-3593
Phone: 603-862-2200
Fax: 603-862-4876
Web site: www.nhsbdc.org

New Jersey
Rutgers University
49 Bleeker Street
Newark, NJ 07102-1993

Phone: 973-353-1927
Fax: 973-353-1110
Web site: www.njsbdc.com/

New Mexico
Santa Fe Community College
6401 Richards Avenue
Santa Fe, NM 87508-4887
Phone: 505-428-1362
Fax: 505-428-1469
Web site: www.nmsbdc.org

New York
State University of New York
Corporate Woods, 3rd Floor
Albany, NY 12246-0001
Phone: 518-443-5398
Fax: 518-443-5275
Web site: www.nyssbdc.org

North Carolina
University of North Carolina
5 West Hargett Street, Suite 600
Raleigh, NC 27601-1348
Phone: 919-715-7272
Fax: 919-715-7777
Web site: www.sbtdc.org

North Dakota
University of North Dakota
1600 E. Century Avenue, Suite 2
Bismarck, ND 58501
Phone: 701-328-5375
Fax: 701-328-5381
Web site: www.ndsbdc.org

Ohio
Ohio Department of Development
128th Floor

PO Box 1001
Columbus, OH 43216-1001
Phone: 614-466-2711
Fax: 614-466-0829
Web site: www.ohiosbdc.org

Oklahoma

Southeast Oklahoma State University
1405 N. 4th Avenue, PMB 2584
Durant, OK 74701-0609
Phone: 580-745-2877 x 2955
Fax: 580-745-7471
Web site: www.osbdc.org

Oregon

Lane Community College
99 West Tenth Avenue, Suite 390
Eugene, OR 97401-3015
Phone: 541-463-5250
Fax: 541-345-6006
Web site: www.bizcenter.org

Pennsylvania

University of Pennsylvania
The Wharton School
3733 Spruce Street, Vance Hall, 4th Floor
Philadelphia, PA 19104-6374
Phone: 215-898-1219
Fax: 215-573-2135
Web site: http://pasbdc.org

Puerto Rico

Inter-American University of Puerto Rico
Union Plaza Building, Suite 1000
416 Ponce de Leon Avenue, 10th Floor
Hato Rey, PR 00918
Phone: 787-763-6811
Fax: 787-763-6875
Web site: www.prsbdc.org

Rhode Island
Johnson and Wales University
270 Weybosset Street, 4th Floor
Providence, RI 02903
Phone: 401-598-2704
Fax: 401-598-2722
Web site: www.risbdc.org

South Carolina
University of South Carolina
Moore School of Business
1710 College Street, Hipp Building
Columbia, SC 29208-9980
Phone: 803-777-4907
Fax: 803-777-4403
Web site: http://scsbdc.moore.sc.edu

South Dakota
University of South Dakota
Beacom School of Business
414 East Clark Street, Patterson Hall
Vermillion, SD 57069
Phone: 605-677-5287
Fax: 605-677-5427
Web site: www.sdsbdc.org

Tennessee
Middle Tennessee State University
615 Memorial Boulevard
Murfreesboro, TN 37132
Phone: 615-849-9999
Fax: 615-217-8548
Web site: www.tsbdc.org

Texas
University of Houston
2302 Fannin, Suite 200
Houston, TX 77002
Phone: 713-752-8444

Fax: 713-756-1500
Web site: http://sbdcnetwork.uh.edu

Dallas County Community College
1402 Corinth Street, Suite 2111
Dallas, TX 75215
Phone: 214-860-5835
Fax: 214-860-5813
Web site: www.ntsbdc.org

Texas Tech University
2579 South Loop 289, Suite 114
Lubbock, TX 79423-1637
Phone: 806-745-3973
Fax: 806-745-6207
Web site: www.nwtsbdc.org

University of Texas—San Antonio
501 West Durango Boulevard
San Antonio, TX 78207-4415
Phone: 210-458-2450
Fax: 210-458-2425
Web site: www.txsbdc.org

Utah
Salt Lake Community College
9750 South 300 West—LHM
Salt Lake City, UT 84070
Phone: 801-957-3481
Fax: 801-957-2007
Web site: www.utahsbdc.org/

Vermont
Vermont Technical College
PO Box 188, 1 Main Street
Randolph Center, VT 05061-0188
Phone: 802-728-9101
Fax: 802-728-3026
Web site: www.vtsbdc.org

Virgin Islands
University of the Virgin Islands
8000 Nisky Center, Suite 720
Charlotte Amalie
St. Thomas, VI 00802-5804
Phone: 340-776-3206
Fax: 340-775-3756
Web site: http://sbdcvi.org

Virginia
George Mason University
Mason Enterprise Center
4031 University Drive, Suite 200
Fairfax, VA 22030-3409
Phone: 703-277-7727
Fax: 703-352-8518
Web site: www.virginiasbdc.org

Washington
Washington State University
534 E. Spokane Falls Blvd.
PO Box 1495
Spokane, WA 99210-1495
Phone: 509-358-7765
Fax: 509-358-7764
Web site: www.wsbdc.org

West Virginia
West Virginia Development Office
1900 Kanawha Blvd. E.
Charleston, WV 25305
Phone: 304-558-2960
Fax: 304-558-0127
Web site: www.sbdcwv.org

Wisconsin
University of Wisconsin
432 North Lake Street, Room 423
Madison, WI 53706

Phone: 608-263-7794
Fax: 608-263-7830
Web site: www.wisconsinsbdc.org

Wyoming
University of Wyoming
1000 E. University, Dept. 3922
Laramie, WY 82979
Phone: 307-766-3505
Fax: 307-766-3406
Web site: www.uwyo.edu/sbdc

Appendix C: Government Grants

The Federal Commons
www.grants.gov
Internet grants management portal serving the grantee organization community.

The Catalog of Federal Domestic Assistance
www.cfda.gov/default.htm

Grant Writing Tips
www.afterschool.gov

Department of Commerce's Federal Grants Page
www.osec.doc.gov/osdbu/faq.htm

The Department of Education's (ED) Portal Site for Electronic Grants
www.gapsweb.rd.gov

Department of Health Resources and Services Administration (HRSA)
www.hrsa.govgrants/default.htm

Department of Justice—Ten Grants
www.doj.gov/10grants/

Department of Labor (DOL)—Employment and Training Administration: Welfare-to-Work Grants Listing by State
www.doleta.gov

Department of Transportation—Federal Highway Administration—Universities and Grants Programs
www.nih.fhwa.dot.gov/home.aspx

HRSA—Office of Rural Health Policy—Grants
www.hrsa.gov/grants/

Department of Labor—Grant and Contract Information
www.dol.gov/dol/grants2.htm

Department of Transportation (DOT)—Hazardous Materials Emergency Preparedness (HMEP) Grant Program
www.hazmat.dot.gov/training/state/hmep/hmep.htm

EPA's Environmental Research Grant Announcements
www.es.epa.gov/ncerga/rfa/

Housing and Urban Development (HUD)—Grants
www.hud.gov/grants/index.cfm

GrantsNet—U.S. Department of Health and Human Services
www.hhs.gov/grantsnet/

NIH—Grants and Funding Opportunities
www.grants.nih.gov/grants/index

National Oceanic and Atmospheric Administration (NOAA)—Business and Grants Opportunities
www.noaa.gov/business.html

NOAA Sponsored National Sea Grant (Link to NOAA's page on National Sea Grants) www.nsgo.seagrant.org/

NOAA's National Marine Fisheries Service—Alaska Region—Grants Information
www.fakr.noaa.gov/omi/grants/default.htm

National Park Service (NPS)—Grants and Tax Credits
www.cr.nps.gov/nagpra/grants/index.htm

National Science Foundation (NSF)—Overview of Grants and Awards
www.nsf.gov/funding/research_edu_community.jsp

Office of Electronic Commerce—Grants
www.egov.gov

Office of Naval Research—Grants, Contracts, and Acquisition
www.onr.navy.mil/02/

Appendix D: Useful IRS Tax Publications

Number	Subject
SS-4	Application for Employer Identification Number
Sch C	Profit or Loss from Business—Sole Proprietor
Sch SE	Computation of Social Security Self-Employment Tax
1040ES	Estimated Tax for Individuals
15	Employers Tax Guide (Circular E)
334	Tax Guide for Small Business
505	Tax Withholding and Estimated Tax
533	Self-Employment Tax
534	Depreciation
535	Business Expense
538	Accounting Periods and Methods
539	Employment Taxes (Defines an Employee)
541	Tax Information on Partnerships
542	Tax Information on Corporations
552	Recordkeeping for Individuals
583	Information for Business Taxpayers
587	Business Use of the Home
589	Tax information on S Corporations
917	Business Use of a Car

Glossary

Accounts Payable: Trade accounts of businesses representing obligations to pay for goods and services received.

Accounts Receivable: Trade accounts of businesses representing money due for goods sold or services rendered evidenced by notes, statements, invoices, or other written evidence of a present obligation.

Accounting: The recording, classifying, summarizing, and interpreting in a significant manner and in terms of money, transactions, and events of a financial character.

Applet: A small Java program that can be embedded in an HTML page. Applets differ from full-fledged Java applications in that they are not allowed to access certain resources on the local computer, such as files and serial devices (modems, printers, etc.), and are prohibited from communicating with most other computers across a network. The current rule is that an applet can only make an Internet connection to the computer from which the applet was sent.

Assumptions: The act of assuming/undertaking another's debts or obligations.

Backbone: A high-speed line or series of connections that forms a major pathway within a network. The term is relative as a backbone in a small network will likely be much smaller than many non-backbone lines in a large network.

Bandwidth: How much data you can send through a connection. Usually measured in bits-per-second. A full page of English text is about 16,000 bits. A fast modem can move about 15,000 bits in one second. Full-motion, full-screen video would require roughly 10,000,000 bits-per-second, depending on compression.

Bankruptcy: A condition in which a business cannot meet its debt obligations and petitions a federal district court for either re-organization of its debts or liquidation of its assets. In the action, the property of a debtor is taken over by a receiver or trustee in bankruptcy for the benefit of the creditors. This action is conducted as prescribed by the National Bankruptcy Act, and may be voluntary or involuntary.

223

Baud: In common usage the baud rate of a modem is how many bits it can send or receive per second. Technically, baud is the number of times per second that the carrier signal shifts value—for example a 1200 bit-per-second modem actually runs at 300 baud, but it moves 4 bits per baud (4 x 300 = 1200 bits per second).

Breakeven Point: The breakeven point in any business is that point at which the volume of sales or revenues exactly equals total expenses—the point at which there is neither a profit nor loss—under varying levels of activity. The breakeven point tells the manager what level of output or activity is required before the firm can make a profit; it reflects the relationship between costs, volume, and profits.

Browser: A client program (software) that is used to look at various kinds of Internet resources.

Business Birth: Formation of a new establishment or enterprise.

Business Death: Voluntary or involuntary closure of a firm or establishment.

Business Dissolution: For enumeration purposes, the absence from any current record of a business that was present in a prior time period.

Business Failure: The closure of a business causing a loss to at least one creditor.

Business Plan: A comprehensive planning document that clearly describes the business developmental objective of an existing or proposed business applying for assistance in SBA's 8(a) or lending programs. The plan outlines what and how and from where the resources needed to accomplish the objective will be obtained and utilized.

Business Start: For enumeration purposes, a business with a name or similar designation that did not exist in a prior time period.

Canceled Loan: The annulment or rescission of an approved loan prior to disbursement.

Capital: Assets less liabilities, representing the ownership interest in a business; a stock of accumulated goods, especially at a specified time and in contrast to income received during a specified time period; accumulated goods devoted to the production of goods; and accumulated possessions calculated to bring income.

Capital Expenditures: Business spending on additional plant equipment and inventory.

Capitalized Property: Personal property of the agency that has an average dollar value of $300.00 or more and a life expectancy of one year or more. Capitalized property shall be depreciated annually over the expected useful life to the agency.

Cash Discount: An incentive offered by the seller to encourage the buyer to pay within a stipulated time. For example, if the terms are 2/10/N 30, the buyer may deduct 2 percent from the amount of the invoice (if paid within ten days); otherwise, the full amount is due in thirty days.

Cash Flow: An accounting presentation showing how much of the cash generated by the business remains after both expenses (including interest) and principal repayment on financing are paid. A projected cash flow statement indicates whether the business will have cash to pay its expenses, loans, and make a profit. Cash flows can be calculated for any given period of time, normally done on a monthly basis.

Certificate Authority: An issuer of Security Certificates used in SSL connections.

Charge-Off: An accounting transaction removing an uncollectible balance from the active receivable accounts.

Charged Off Loan: An uncollectible loan for which the principal and accrued interest were removed from the receivable accounts.

Closing: Actions and procedures required to affect the documentation and disbursement of loan funds after the application has been approved and the execution of all required documentation and its filing and recording where required.

Closed Loan: Any loan for which funds have been disbursed and all required documentation has been executed, received, and reviewed. For statistical purposes, first or total disbursement is counted as a closed loan.

Collateral: Something of value—securities, evidence of deposit, or other property—pledged to support the repayment of an obligation.

Collateral Document: A legal document covering the item(s) pledged as collateral on a loan (i.e., note, mortgages, assignment, etc.).

Consortium: A coalition of organizations, such as banks and corporations, set up to fund ventures requiring large capital resources.

Corporation: A group of persons granted a state charter legally recognizing them as a separate entity having its own rights, privileges, and liabilities distinct from those of its members. The process of incorporating should be completed with the state's secretary of state or state corporate counsel, and usually requires the services of an attorney.

Compromise: The settlement of a claim resulting from a defaulted loan for less than the full amount due. Compromise settlement is a procedure available for use only in instances where the government cannot collect the full amount due within a reasonable time, by enforced collection proceedings, or where the cost of such proceedings would not justify such effort.

Contingent Liability: A potential obligation that may be incurred dependent upon the occurrence of a future event. Two examples are: (1) the liability of an endorser or guarantor of a note if the primary borrower fails to pay as agreed and (2) the liability that would be incurred if a pending lawsuit is resolved in the other party's favor.

Costs: Money obligated for goods and services received during a given period of time, regardless of when ordered or whether paid for.

Credit Rating: A grade assigned to a business concern to denote the net worth and credit standing to which the concern is entitled in the opinion of the rating agency as a result of its investigation.

Debenture: Debt instrument evidencing the holder's right to receive interest and principal installments from the named obligor. Applies to all forms of unsecured, long-term debt evidenced by a certificate of debt.

Debt Capital: Business financing that normally requires periodic interest payments and repayment of the principal within a specified time.

Debt Financing: The provision of long-term loans to small business concerns in exchange for debt securities or a note.

Deed of Trust: A document under seal, which, when delivered, transfers a present interest in property. May be held as collateral.

Defaults: The nonpayment of principal and/or interest on the due date as provided by the terms and conditions of the note.

Deferred Loan: Loans whose principal and or interest installments are postponed for a specified period of time.

Disbursement: The actual payout to borrower of loan funds, in whole or part. It may be received during the closing or follow it.

Domain Name: The unique name that identifies an Internet site. Domain names always have two or more parts, separated by dots. The part on the left is the most specific, and the part on the right is the most general. A given machine may have more than one domain name, but a given domain name points to only one machine. Usually, all of the machines on a given network will have the same thing as the right-hand portion of their domain names. It is also possible for a domain name to exist but not be connected to an actual machine. This is often done so that a group or business can have an Internet e-mail address without having to establish a real Internet site. In these cases, some real Internet machine must handle the mail on behalf of the listed domain name.

DSL: (Digital Subscriber Line)—A method for moving data over regular phone lines. A DSL circuit is much faster than a regular phone connection, and the wires coming into the subscriber's premises are the same (copper) wires used for regular phone service. A DSL circuit must be configured to connect two specific locations, similar to a leased line. A commonly discussed configuration of DSL allows downloads at speeds of up to 1.544 megabits (not megabytes) per second, and uploads at speeds of 128 kilobits per second. This arrangement is called ADSL: "Asymmetric" Digital Subscriber Line. Another common configuration is symmetrical: 384 kilobits per second in both directions. In theory, ADSL allows download speeds of up to 9 megabits per second and upload speeds of up to 640 kilobits per second. DSL is now a popular alternative to Leased Lines and ISDN, being faster than ISDN and less costly than traditional Leased Lines.

Earning Power: The demonstrated ability of a business to earn a profit, over time, while following good accounting practices. When a business shows a reasonable profit on invested capital after fully maintaining the business property, appropriately compensating its owner and employees, servicing its obligations, and fully recognizing its costs, the business may be said to have demonstrated earning power. Demonstrated earning power is the foremost test of the business risk in pressing upon an application for a loan.

Enterprise: Aggregation of all establishments owned by a parent company. An enterprise can consist of a single, independent establishment or it can include subsidiaries or other branch establishments under the same ownership and control.

Entrepreneur: One who assumes the financial risk of the initiation, operation, and management of a given business or undertaking.

Equity: An ownership interest in a business.

Equity Financing: The provision of funds for capital or operating expenses in exchange for capital stock, stock purchase warrants, and options in the business financed without any guaranteed return, but with the opportunity to share in the company's profits. Equity financing includes long-term subordinated securities containing stock options and/or warrants. Utilized in SBIC financing activities.

Equity Partnership: A limited partnership arrangement for providing startup and seed capital to businesses.

Escrow Accounts: Funds placed in trust with a third party by a borrower for a specific purpose and to be delivered to the borrower only upon the fulfillment of certain conditions.

Establishment: A single-location business unit, which may be independent—called a single-establishment enterprise—or owned by a parent enterprise.

Financial Report: Report commonly required from an applicant request for financial assistance. For example: Balance Sheet—A report of the status of a firm's assets, liabilities, and owner's equity at a given time. Income Statement—A report of revenue and expense that shows the results of business operations or net income for a specified period of time.

Financing: New funds provided to a business, by either loans, purchase of debt securities, or capital stock.

Flow Chart: A graphical representation for the definition, analysis, or solution of a problem, in which symbols are used to represent operations, data, flow, equipment, etc.

Foreclosure: The act by the mortgagee or trustee upon default in the payment of interest or principal of a mortgage of enforcing payment of the debt by selling the underlying security.

Franchising: A continuing relationship in which the franchisor provides a licensed privilege to the franchisee to do business and offers assistance in organizing, training, merchandising, marketing, and managing in return for a consideration. Franchising is a form of business by which the owner (franchisor) of a product, service, or method obtains distribution through affiliated dealers (franchisees). The product, method, or service being marketed is usually identified by the franchisor's brand name, and the holder of the privilege (franchisee) is often given exclusive access to a defined geographical area.

Guaranteed Loan: A loan made and serviced by a lending institution under agreement that a governmental agency will purchase the guaranteed portion if the borrower defaults.

Hardware: A term used to describe the mechanical, electrical, and electronic elements of a data processing system.

Hazard Insurance: Insurance required showing lender as loss payee covering certain risks on real and personal property used for securing loans.

Incubator: A facility designed to encourage entrepreneurship and minimize obstacles to new business formation and growth, particularly for high technology firms, by housing a number of fledgling enterprises that share an array of services. These shared services may include meeting areas, secretarial services, accounting services, research libraries, on-site financial and management counseling, and word processing facilities.

Independent and Qualified Public Accountants: Public accountants are independent when neither they nor any of their family have a material, direct, or indirect financial interest in the borrower other than as an accountant. They are qualified, unless there is contrary evidence, when they are either (1) certified, licensed, or otherwise registered if so required by the state in which they work, or (2) have worked as a public accountant for at least five years and are accepted by SBA.

Innovation: Introduction of a new idea into the marketplace in the form of a new product or service or an improvement in organization or process.

Insolvency: The inability of a borrower to meet financial obligations as they mature or having insufficient assets to pay legal debts.

Interest: An amount paid a lender for the use of funds.

Internet: Any time you connect two or more networks together, you have an internet—as in inter-national or inter-state.

Intranet: A private network inside a company or organization that uses the same kinds of software that you would find on the public Internet, but that is only for internal use. As the Internet has become more popular, many of the tools used on the Internet are being used in private networks. For example, many companies have Web servers that are available only to employees. Note that an Intranet may not actually be an internet—it may simply be a network.

Inverse Order of Maturity: When payments are received from borrowers that are larger than the authorized repayment schedules, the overpayment is credited to the final installments of the principal, which reduces the maturity of the loan and does not affect the original repayment schedule.

Investment Banking: Businesses specializing in the formation of capital. This is done by outright purchase and sale of securities offered by the issuer, standby underwriting, or "best efforts selling."

Invitation for Bids: Formal solicitations for offerings to perform procurements by competitive bids when the specifications describe the requirements of the government clearly, accurately, and completely, but avoiding unnecessarily restrictive specifications or requirements that might unduly limit the number of bidders.

Job Description: A written statement listing the elements of a particular job or occupation (e.g., purpose, duties, equipment used, qualifications, training, physical and mental demands, working conditions, etc.).

Judgment: Judicial determination of the existence of an indebtedness or other legal liability.

Lease: A contract between the owner (lessor) and the tenant (leassee) stating the conditions under which the tenant may occupy or use the property.

Legal Rate of Interest: The maximum rate of interest fixed by the laws of the various states, which a lender may charge a borrower for the use of money.

Lending Institution: Any institution, including a commercial bank, savings and loan association, commercial finance company, or other lender qualified to participate with SBA in the making of loans.

Lien: A charge upon or security interest in real or personal property maintained to ensure the satisfaction of a debt or duty ordinarily arising by operation of law.

Liquidation: The disposal, at maximum prices, of the collateral securing a loan and the voluntary and enforced collection of the remaining loan balance from the obligators and/or guarantors.

Liquidation Value: The net value realizable in the sale (ordinarily a forced sale) of a business or a particular asset.

Loan Agreement: Agreement to be executed by borrower, containing pertinent terms, conditions, covenants, and restrictions.

Loan Payoff Amount: The total amount of money needed to meet a borrower's obligation on a loan. It is arrived at by accruing gross interest for one day and multiplying this figure by the number of days that exist between the date of the last repayment and the date on which the loan is to be completely paid off. This amount, known as accrued interest, is combined with the latest principal and escrow balances that are applicable to what is now referred to as the loan payoff amount. In the case where prepaid interest exceeds the accrued interest, the latter is subtracted from the former and the difference is used to reduce the total amount owed.

Loss Rate: A rate developed by comparing the ratio of total loans charged off to the total loans disbursed from inception of the program to the present date.

Markup: Markup is the difference between invoice cost and selling price. It may be expressed either as a percentage of the selling price or the cost price and is supposed to cover all the costs of doing business plus a profit. Whether markup is based on the selling price or the cost price, the base is always equal to 100 percent.

Maturity: As applied to securities and commercial paper, the period end date when payment of principal is due.

Maturity Extension: Extensions of payment beyond the original period established for repayment of a loan.

Merger: A combination of two or more corporations wherein the dominant unit absorbs the passive ones, the former continuing operation usually under the same name. In a consolidation, two units combine and are succeeded by a new corporation, usually with a new title.

Mortgage: An instrument giving legal title to secure the repayment of a loan made by the mortgagee (lender). There are two types: (1) title theory—operates as a transfer of the legal title of the property to the mortgagee, and (2) lien theory—creates a lien upon the property in favor of the mortgagee.

Negotiation: The face-to-face process used by local unions and the employer to exchange their views on those matters involving personnel policies and practices or other matters affecting the working conditions of employees in the unit and reduced to a written binding agreement. Used also by contracting officers to reach agreement with potential contractors.

Net Worth: Property owned (assets), minus debts and obligations owed (liabilities), is the owner's equity (net worth).

Notes and Accounts Receivable: A secured or unsecured receivable evidenced by a note or open account arising from activities involving liquidation and disposal of loan collateral.

Obligations: Technically defined as "amount of orders placed, contracts awarded, services received, and similar transactions during a given period, which will require payments during the same or a future period."

Ordinary Interest: Simple interest based on a year of 360 days, contrasting with exact interest having a base year of 365 days.

Partnership: A legal relationship existing between two or more persons contractually associated as joint principals in a business.

Prime Rate: Interest rate, which is charged to business borrowers having the highest credit ratings for short term borrowing.

Pro-Net: An Internet-based database of information of small, disadvantaged, 8(a), and women-owned businesses seeking procurement contracts.

Product Liability: Type of tort or civil liability that applies to product manufacturers and sellers.

Proprietorship: The most common legal form of business ownership; about 85 percent of all small businesses are proprietorships. The liability of the owner is unlimited in this form of ownership.

Ratio: Denotes relationships of items within and between financial statements (e.g., current ratio, quick ratio, inventory turnover ratio, and debt/net worth ratios).

Request for Proposals: Solicitations for offerings for competitive negotiated procurements when it is impossible to draft an invitation for bids containing adequate detailed description of the required property and services. There are fifteen circumstances in the Federal Acquisition Regulations (FAR) that permit negotiated procurements.

Return on Investment: The amount of profit (return) based on the amount of resources (funds) used to produce it. Also the ability of a given investment to earn a return for its use.

Secondary Market: Those who purchase an interest in a loan from an original lender, such as banks, institutional investors, insurance companies, credit unions, and pension funds.

Service Corps of Retired Executives (SCORE): Retired and working successful business persons who volunteer to render assistance in counseling, training, and guiding small business clients.

Small Business Development Center (SBDC): The SBDC is a university-based center for the delivery of joint government, academic, and private sector services for the benefit of small business and the national welfare. It is committed to the development and productivity of business and the economy in specific geographical regions.

Turnover (Business): Turnover is the number of times that an average inventory of goods is sold during a fiscal year or some designated period. Care must be taken to ensure that the average inventory and net sales are both reduced to the same denominator; that is, divide inventory at cost into sales at cost or divide inventory at selling price into sales at selling price. Do not mix cost price with selling price. The turnover, when accurately computed, is one measure of the efficiency of a business.

Undelivered Orders: The amount of orders for goods and services outstanding for which the liability has not yet accrued. For practical purposes, represents obligations incurred for which goods have not been delivered or services not performed.

Venture Capital: Money used to support new or unusual commercial undertakings; equity, risk, or speculative capital. This funding is provided to new or existing firms that exhibit above-average growth rates, a significant potential for market expansion, and the need for additional financing for business maintenance or expansion.

References

Internal Revenue Service (2008). *Tax information for* businesses—
www.irs.gov/businesses/index.html

Small Business Administration (2008). *Small business planner*—
www.sba.gov/smallbusinessplanner/index.html

U. S. Department of Health and Human Services (2008). *Find grant information*—
www.Grants.gov/applicants/applicants.jsp

About the Authors

David P. Hale, PhD, is the founder and CEO of HiPer Solutions, a premier global provider of corporate leadership consulting and training. He holds an MBA in managerial leadership, an MA and PhD in industrial and organizational psychology, and has over twenty-five years of experience in the fields of leadership, organizational communication, and business development. Dave is a frequent speaker at professional organizations and on the faculty of Northcentral and Webster Universities, where he teaches organizational psychology and business management courses. He is also featured in *Straight Talk: Corporate America's 10 Most Requested Speakers & Trainers*, published by Insight Publishing. He can be reached via the Internet at www. hipercoaching.com or e-mail at DrDave@ HiPerCoaching.com.

Barbara Lyngarkos, MBA, is the founder and CEO of Executary, Inc., a provider of business incubation services. She holds an MBA in individualized studies, and is a PhD candidate in the e-commerce program at Northcentral University. Barbara has over twenty-five years of operational expertise focusing on business development. Recently fulfilling a long-time dream, Barbara has formed The Wool Garden, an e-commerce venture serving the quilting and craft industries. She can be reached via the Internet at www.thewoolgarden.com or e-mail at Barbara@ thewoolgarden.com.

Timothy P. Maxwell II is the owner of AFC Group, LLC, a real estate and business management firm. He has been passionate about real estate investing for several years while completing deals worth several millions of dollars. Timothy graduated from the University of South Carolina with a degree in real estate and is currently an MBA student with Webster University. He can be reached at afcgrouppllc@aol.com and www.webuysumter.com.

Michael B. Meek, MSM, is founder and CEO of M. B. Meek Consultants, a provider of leadership and cultural development consulting since the 1980s both in the United States and abroad. Mike is presently a PhD candidate in the organizational leadership program with Northcentral University. He has personally worked with over thirty thousand people throughout the last two decades implementing his change management process across a variety of industry sectors. Mike has authored several management training programs, which can be seen at www.mbmeek.com. He can be reached at mike@mbmeek.com and 800-559-MEEK(6335).

Robert T. Uda, MBA, is the founder and president of Bob Uda and Associates, a counterterrorism research company. He is Certified Manager, Board of Regents Vice-Chairman for the Institute of Certified Professional Managers, and has over forty years of experience in the fields of career development. Bob is internationally recognized for community service, listed in forty-six *Who's Who* publications, and has authored fourteen books with his latest titled *Guerrilla Networking: The Best Way to Capture and Keep Great Jobs*, published by iUniverse, Inc. Bob is presently a PhD candidate in Business Administration at Northcentral University. He can be reached at bobuda@roadrunner.com.

Business Startup Goals:

- ✓ Concept development
- ✓ Web site design
- ✓ Develop contacts
- ✓ Financing
- ✓ Office setup
- ✓ Hire employees
- ✓ Franchise or develop my own
- ✓ Management issues
- ✓ Business plan
- ✓ Marketing plan

Start Here Today:
www.HiPerCoaching.com

Are you checking all of your business startup blocks? Why go the route of so many entrepreneurs who fail their first year due to poor planning. At HiPer Solutions, we know business success. We are entrepreneurs who coach entrepreneurs on all areas of the startup process.

Visit our Web site today—**www.HiPerCoaching.com**—to learn more, do more, and achieve more business success. Find out about our entrepreneur coaching program that has been taught around the world. Now, you can receive the same personal coaching services that many entrepreneurs have received, who are now millionaires.

HiPer Solutions
"Success on Demand"
www.HiPerCoaching.com

978-0-595-49647-1
0-595-49647-4

www.ingramcontent.com/pod-product-compliance
Lightning Source LLC
Chambersburg PA
CBHW020741180526
45163CB00001B/304